Merry Christmas, Gerry.
1984
Phil Riley Jr

JACKSON

The Empire Block was one of the early business blocks in Jackson. It is believed to have been in existence on Main Street as early as 1849 and was still standing into the late 1860s. Webb and Butler's, the confectionery store on the left, provided refreshments to the 1854 Republican convention. Courtesy, Jackson Citizen Patriot

JACKSON

AN ILLUSTRATED HISTORY
BRIAN DEMING

"PARTNERS IN PROGRESS"
BY
PATRICIA McENROE KOSCHIK

PRODUCED IN COOPERATION WITH
THE GREATER JACKSON CHAMBER
OF COMMERCE
WINDSOR PUBLICATIONS, INC.
WOODLAND HILLS, CALIFORNIA

Windsor Publications, Inc. — History Books Division
Publisher: John M. Phillips
Staff for *Jackson: An Illustrated History*
Editor/Picture Editor: Julie Jaskol
Editorial Director, Corporate Biographies: Karen Story
Design Director: Alexander D'Anca
Assistant Director, Corporate Biographies: Phyllis Gray
Editor, Corporate Biographies: Judy Hunter
Editorial Assistants: Patricia Buzard, Lonnie Pham, Pat Pittman
Marketing Director: Ellen Kettenbeil
Sales Manager: Robert Moffitt
Sales Representatives: Cal Young, Al Crowell

Library of Congress Data
Deming, Brian, 1954-
Jackson: an illustrated history
"Produced in cooperation with the
    Greater Jackson Chamber of
    Commerce"—T.p. verso.
Bibliography: p. 130 Includes index.
    1. Jackson (Mich.)—History. 2.
Jackson (Mich.)—Description. 3.
Jackson (Mich.)—Industries. I.
Koschik, Patricia McEnroe.
Partners in progress. 1984. II.
Greater Jackson Chamber of
Commerce. III. Title.
F574.J14D46   1984977.4'28   84-20913
ISBN 0-89781-113-5

4

CONTENTS

TO MY MOTHER AND FATHER

ACKNOWLEDGMENTS

Facing page: *Loomis Park was the first large neighborhood park in Jackson, given to the city by Peter B. Loomis in 1902. Loomis was a prominent 19th century Jackson civic leader who played many roles in Jackson political and business life. Born in 1820, he came to Jackson in 1843 and entered a dry goods business. He later owned a flour mill, became senior partner in a banking firm, led the movement to supply natural gas to the city, managed a railroad, edited the Jackson* Daily Press, *and served as mayor, state legislator, and fire chief. Courtesy, Frank Machnik Collection*

I am grateful for the help of many people in the preparation of this book. In particular, I appreciate the advice of Ken Wyatt, Glenn Atkin, Max Brail, Millie Hadwin, and Linnea Loftis. They read drafts of each chapter and offered thoughtful criticisms. In my search for information and pictures, I received much assistance from staff people at various institutions and businesses including the *Jackson Citizen Patriot,* Consumers Power Company, the Jackson District Library, the Bentley Historical Library at the University of Michigan, the Michigan Space Center, the Clarke Historical Library at Central Michigan University, the State of Michigan Archives, Jackson Community College, Spring Arbor College, and the Ella Sharp Museum. There were also many private individuals who allowed me access to their collections of historical photographs and materials. These people include Frances Williams, B.W. Bartus, Thomas A. Johnson, Lloyd Ganton, Richard Babcock, Dr. Byrne M. Daly, and Wilma Kerwin. Mary E. Abbott and Gladys Porter were kind enough to assist in providing color photographs for this book. Finally, I want to thank Carol Damioli. Her encouragement and patience throughout helped prevent a difficult project from becoming an ordeal.

INTRODUCTION

The people of Jackson entered the decade of the 1980s with a good deal of uncertainty about their town's future. Jackson once dwarfed neighboring towns such as Lansing and Ann Arbor. Now those towns were much bigger. Not only that, they seemed more prosperous and assured of a more promising future. In Jackson two major factories, Clark Equipment and Goodyear Tire, closed within one year of each other. Other smaller companies had left or were expanding elsewhere. A once-thriving downtown was dotted with empty storefronts. While the county as a whole was growing, the city was not. Indeed, the population of the city was shrinking.

Jackson's troubles were not so different from those of many American communities, but in Jackson the problems seem to have been a little worse and the solutions a little more elusive.

Inevitably, there is a desire to return things to the way they used to be. I was struck by this attitude when I came to Jackson in late 1979. The failures of the present seemed to make the past ever more happy and prosperous.

This book is an attempt to set the record straight about the way things used to be. It is not meant as an invitation to turn back the clock but to meet the future with a better understanding of the past. Maybe within this book there are lessons for tomorrow. History is just an exercise in trivia if it is not used to understand the present and anticipate the future.

Of course this book records the actions of the rich and powerful, those who left their names on buildings and parks and streets. But it is also a history of those without wealth or power who worked in the factory or in the home to make life better for themselves and their children. Among those people were two grandparents I never knew — Wilbur Deming, a tradesman and upholsterer and the son of a Jackson blacksmith, and Maude Embury Deming, mother of four children and daughter of a lumber and railroad man. They lived on E. Michigan Avenue just east of the city and did their best to survive the Great Depression. They too, and thousands like them, made Jackson's history and helped weave the texture of the community.

This history is not strictly chronological. It is a topical

history, each chapter devoted to a general subject. The first chapter examines Jackson's settlement. The second traces the history of religious and educational institutions as well as newspapers, radio, and television. The third chapter is an outline of Jackson's business and industrial past. The fourth chapter summarizes life in Jackson outside of the workplace: its parks, recreation, entertainment, athletics, and theater. The final chapter traces the community as it has changed through the years — its architecture, size, and people.

One note of clarification: the name of Jackson's main thoroughfare has been changed several times. I often used the name Michigan Avenue, the modern name, even though contemporaries may have recognized it as Main Street or St. Joseph Street.

While this history focuses on the city, it includes much about what went on outside the city, within the county. I know as well as anyone that there is much that is missing, particularly histories of outlying villages. I leave that to other historians.

I also leave to others the duty of ferreting out and correcting errors that may have crept into this book. Diligent as I was in honestly weighing the credibility of sources and in resolving conflicting accounts, some mistakes no doubt remain.

On the whole, however, I believe this history is accurate and fair. I hope it is also interesting and enlightening.

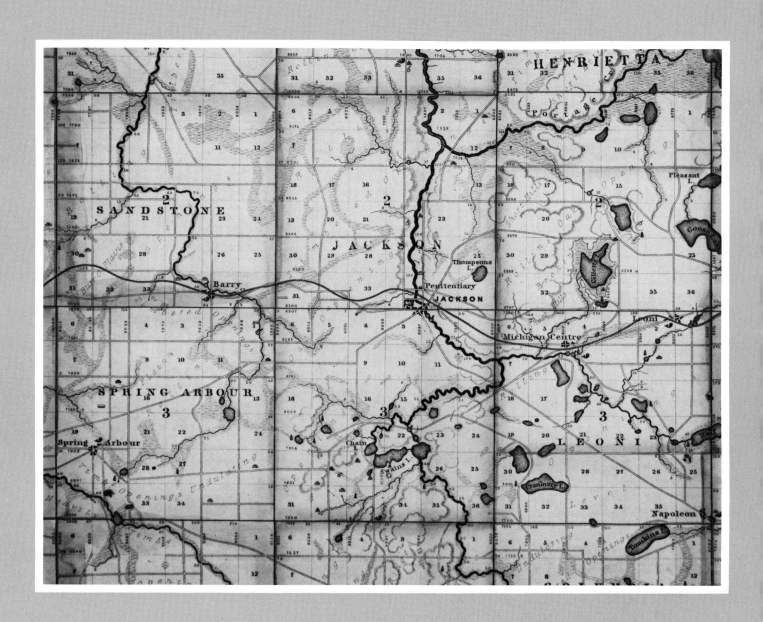

CHAPTER ONE

From Blackman's Location to Jackson

Rifle shots shattered the stillness of the summer morning in the Michigan wilderness. The blasts echoed over oaks, lindens, maples, over an Indian campground, over a stream the Indians called the Washtenong Sepe. This was the dawn of July 4, 1829, and the awakening of a place that would be called Jackson.

Three men greeted the day with rifle shots fired, not in anger, but in celebration. They were Pewytum, an Indian guide, and two white men, Alexander Laverty, a guide, and Horace Blackman, a 28-year-old prospective settler. The three had reached this place after a hot, two-day hike from the frontier hamlet of Ann Arbor. Near sunset of the second day, they reached the east bank of a river, the Indian name for which meant "clear, swift stream running over a bed of pebbles." White men had a less descriptive, less accurate name for this modest stream: the Grand River.

The three forded the stream at a point near where Trail Street would someday bridge the river. They camped that July 3 near the west bank. To the north lay an Indian cornfield; to the west rose a range of hills; to the south heavy timber.

This was the place Blackman knew he wanted to make his home. The next day they celebrated the discovery of the location as well as the 53rd anniversary of American independence. After a sunrise rifle salute, Laverty made a speech in Potawatomie and then in English. The three then toasted the holiday with water from the river. Pewytum finished the impromptu ceremony with a rifle shot.

Like many who came to settle Michigan, Blackman was from New York. Back in Tioga County he had heard reports about Michigan, particularly from Jonathon Stratton, a surveyor who came to Michigan in 1826 and quickly saw the direction of Michigan's growth. Stratton would prove to be a powerful influence on the founding and shaping of Jackson. He wrote to friends in New York about the territory which had largely been bypassed by westward migration.

Widely-read reports early in the 19th century discouraged migration into the area. The reports condemned Michigan as unfarmable wasteland because of its marshes and wet prairies. Stratton saw differently. He wrote encouraging letters about this

Horace Blackman and his scouting party arrived at the west bank of the Grand River on July 3, 1829. Blackman, from Tioga County, New York, staked the first claim in the settlement and returned the following year with a band of settlers. Courtesy, Jackson District Library

territory. Blackman, heartened by Stratton's letters, raised money by selling horses and borrowing from his father, and started for Michigan.

Blackman found Stratton in Ann Arbor, at that time the last western outpost from Detroit and barely holding its own in the thinly settled territory. Stratton told Blackman that a new county would be eventually established west of Washtenaw County. An Indian trail leading west from Ann Arbor crossed the Grand River near the center of the proposed county. A location there would have many advantages. Since roads tended to follow the paths of Indian trails, it would probably be assured a place along a major thoroughfare. Located on a river, it would have access to a source of power for a mill. Being near the center of a county, it could be named county seat, giving it prestige and added commerce as the center of government.

Blackman hired Laverty and Pewytum to guide him west. He found even more advantages than Stratton described. Not one, but at least three and as many as 11 Indian trails came together at that point on the river. Much of the land was elevated and well-drained and thus suitable for farming. There were good supplies of oak and other trees nearby for building and fuel. The river could easily be forded at this point. Blackman returned to Ann Arbor and then Monroe and registered his claim for 160 acres at two dollars an acre.

Not everyone was as excited about the place as Blackman. People in Ann Arbor thought he had picked a spot too far west. They said it would be another 20 years before settlement reached that far.

Russell Blackman, Horace's brother, was also disappointed. He joined Horace in August bringing with him badly needed money. He felt Horace had found a place that was too isolated, but he went along with the decision. The two of them bought oxen and a wagon and hired three men. Together, they made their way to Blackman's claim, cleared land and built a cabin. Built on the corner of what would become Ingham and Trail streets, it was made of logs and covered with split shingles.

They returned to Ann Arbor in October, where Russell stayed to earn money. Horace returned to New York to prepare his family and other settlers for the trip west in the spring. By spring, however, the shaping of the community and even the naming of it would be largely out of his control.

On January 1, 1830, a federal law went into effect making it easier to claim unsettled land. Thus, unbeknownst to the Blackmans, a host of claims were filed for land around the so-called Blackman's Location. Particularly crucial, as far as the Blackmans were concerned, were claims made upstream where the construction of a mill could take away the advantage of waterpower Blackman had counted on. William and Hiram Thompson, Benjamin H. Packard, William J. Moody, Isaiah W. Bennett, E.W. Morgan, and Chauncey C. Lewis were the names of some of these people who, like Blackman, saw the advantages of the location. Anticipating Blackman's plans, Bennett and William Thompson built a dam and a rude sawmill in 1830, upstream from Blackman's claim. It would force Blackman to compromise the plan he had for the village.

That same year, even before any permanent settlers arrived, the place was given an official name. A legislative council of the territory had authorized a road from Sheldon's Corner, later Plymouth, to the mouth of the St. Joseph River on Lake Michigan. Winter was the best time to survey the road because marshes and streams were frozen and easy to cross. Thus, in January, a surveying party and a group of curious Ann Arbor citizens made their way from Ann Arbor to Blackman's hut on the Grand. They arrived on January 14 and had to cut their way into Blackman's windowless, doorless cabin. No less than 14 men crowded into the hut for shelter for two nights. Included in the group were Russell Blackman, Pewytum, Laverty, and Stratton.

The group decided the location needed a name and Stratton and Orrin White of Detroit were called upon to make a recommendation. Their choice: Jacksonburg, in honor of then president Andrew Jackson. The name was adopted enthusiastically with dancing and a chorus of "Yankee Doodle."

According to one story, postal officials gave the settlement the name Jacksonopolis to avoid confusion with other Jacksonburgs in the country. That circumstance only added to confusion, however, and in 1838, townspeople decided to lop off the end of the name altogether. Jacksonburg or Jacksonopolis became simply Jackson.

In the spring of 1830 Blackman returned to the place now called Jacksonburg and by now already noticed by other settlers. He brought with him four wagons and 14 settlers including his wife, his parents, several brothers and sisters, and the families of William DeLand and E.B. Chapman. Despite the attention the place had already received and its evident potential, some of the newcomers were dismayed. Two of the women, Julia Chapman and Lucy Blackman, dutifully prepared and served the first meal at the new home and then, out of sight of the menfolk, "had a

good cry," according to stories later told by the women.

The settlers slept in wagons while flooring was laid in the log cabin and bunks put up. Cooking was done outdoors and clothing dried on log poles. A small barn had to be built for the oxen and the first and only cow in the new settlement so the wolves would not destroy them.

These settlers were soon joined by others and by November 1830, 30 families had come to live at the settlement. Most came from New York, but families also came from Maine, Massachusetts, and Ohio.

The settlers planned a community with St. Joseph Street, later called Main Street and then Michigan Avenue, as the main thoroughfare. According to the new plat, laid out by Jonathon Stratton, the village would be bounded by Trail Street on the north, Franklin Street on the south, Blackstone Street on the west, and the river on the east. Jackson Street was established as the main north-south street with the village square where Jackson and St. Joseph intersected.

Part of St. Joseph Street, named after the major Indian trail in the area, ran through a swamp. The area near the main intersection, where the L.H. Field Department Store would one day be built, was a marsh full of cattails. A small creek also crossed the main street near the planned village square. It was low and swampy from Blackstone Street to Page Avenue and almost impassable in the rainy season until it was paved in 1848.

Worse than its lowness, St. Joseph Street was not along the path of the territorial road that ran from Detroit to Lake Michigan. That road was laid out less than a mile north of the main street, along the path of what would become Ganson Street. The townspeople faced the possibility that travelers east and west would bypass the village. To capture that commerce, two streets were laid out connecting St. Joseph Street with the territorial road; they would eventually be called E. Michigan and Wildwood avenues.

Jacksonburg soon grew as a commercial center. Also, just as Blackman had hoped, the town was declared county seat. A committee whose membership included the ever-present Stratton recommended to the governor the village of Jacksonburg not only as county seat, but as state capitol, promising ten acres on the north side of the settlement for the statehouse square.

The state almost accepted that offer when, in 1847, legislators finally got around to moving the capitol from Detroit. Opposition, largely from Detroit and Marshall, forced a compromise. Lansing, then nothing more than a dam and a log cabin in the woods in Ingham County, was picked over Jackson, by then a thriving town of about 3,000, fourth-largest in the state. A historian, writing in 1881, recalled that Jackson legislators took the decision philosophically: "Though to an extent disappointed, they wisely cast their influence to build up a neighborly county that seemed to have much less natural chance for prosperity." On February 6, 1831, Gov. Lewis Cass declared Jacksonburg the county seat.

As settlers came into the county in the 1830s, the county was broken up into townships. At first, the entire county was governed as Jacksonburg Township. By 1833, when the county board of supervisors first met, the county was split up into four townships: Jacksonburg, Spring Arbor, Napoleon, and Grass Lake. It was still a wild territory. One of the first actions taken by the first supervisors of the county was to offer a $2.50 bounty for the scalp of any full-grown wolf killed within three miles of the dwelling of any white inhabitant.

More people poured into the county and by 1836 the number of townships increased to 10 with the addition of Concord, Hanover, Leoni, East Portage (later Waterloo), West Portage (later Henrietta), and Sandstone townships. These were each carved out of the four original townships. Pulaski, Parma, Tompkins, Rives, Liberty, and Springport townships were organized in 1837. Columbia Township was added in 1839, and Summit, Blackman, and Norvell townships were added in the 1850s.

Of course, from the beginning the settlers were not alone in the wilderness. In fact, Pewytum, Laverty, and Blackman were not alone when they celebrated on that July 4 morning. Their gunfire attracted nearby Indians who came out of curiosity and then feasted with the three on green corn, potatoes, fish, and game. It was a typical gesture of Indians in the area who, despite fears of white settlers, never were a hindrance to the flood of white settlement that was to come.

In the Jackson area, relations between settlers and Indians were often uneasy but never violent. The Indians in Jackson County were, for the most part, Potawatomies. The largest Indian village was near Spring Arbor at what would be the intersection of South Cross and Hammond roads. The village leader, Whap-ca-zeek, had lost a leg fighting white soldiers in the Battle of Tippecanoe. He was nursed back to health by whites and remained friendly toward the newcomers. Settlers told stories of joining Indian celebrations. One, near Brown's Lake, was a wedding party hosted by an Indian named

Tat-a-wa-see-bing who was father of the bride. The "pow-wow," settlers reported, "was the biggest drunk we ever remember of."

The Indians, naturally, were curious about the ways of the intruders, and the settlers, for their part, tried to indoctrinate the natives to new habits. One pioneer woman, Mary DeLand, attempted to make a Christian out of Pewytum. This Indian, who was always polite to the settlers, took a liking to the ruffled shirts the white men wore. Mrs. DeLand saw this and promised him that she would make him a shirt if he would come to Sunday services.

She made him a shirt out of curtain calico and, as promised, he showed up at Sunday services. He wore the shirt, moccasins, and nothing else. Wrote Mrs. DeLand's son Charles years later: "It is said he was not pressed to attend anymore." Beneath the outwardly friendly relations between settlers and Indians, there was uncertainty. To the south was the Black Hawk War, an Indian uprising, and people in Jackson were never sure their neighbors would remain peaceful. And peace was not enough for the settlers who still saw the Indians as obstacles to the advance of civilization. They were annoyed by roving Indians who, they said, would often come upon a cabin and "walk right in and take possession, remaining until they had eaten everything in sight."

Wrote Charles V. DeLand, Jackson historian:

The Indians were not naturally thievish, and yet they had a way of taking things that was in many instances unpleasant and annoying. They were great beggars, and visited the settlers' cabins without warning and insisted on being fed and lodged on cold winter nights. If accommodated they were peaceful and orderly when not under the influence of liquor, and very seldom made trouble. But they were none the less a great nuisance and the people were required to be rid of them.

Get rid of them they did. In two years, 1839 and 1840, the United States cavalry came to Jackson and camped on Moody Hill, near where Ganson Street and Lansing Avenue would intersect. The troops gathered up the Indians in the area, 1,500 according to one estimate, and escorted them to Detroit. From there they were taken by boat with other Indians in the state to Fort Howard, Wisconsin, and resettled. Jackson and Jackson County were nothing more than a few scattered clearings in the woods. There was room for everyone, settlers thought, except the natives.

CHAPTER TWO

Spirit, Mind, and Voice

Facing page: *These boys at the time of their first communion were photographed about 1925 in an eastside studio, later the site of the Polish Legion of American Veterans, at 625 Page Avenue. The boys were most likely from Jackson's predominantly Polish parishes of St. Joseph or St. Stanislaus Kostka. Courtesy, Frank Machnik Collection*

The settlers who came to Jackson brought more with them than what they carried in their wagons. They brought their sense of what a community, and a city, should be. They built institutions to reflect those values. Institutions such as churches, schools, and newspapers would embody the community's spirit, mind, voice, goals, and pride, as well as its divisions, fears, and shortcomings.

Settlers felt a need to establish religious institutions almost as soon as they arrived from New York and New England. Before they could worship in the manner to which they were accustomed, they made do without traditional church buildings and sometimes without proper clergy. Isaiah W. Bennett, a one-time preacher who, it was said, the "strenuousness of pioneer life" had caused to "fall from grace," was one of the first to deliver a sermon in the new settlement. This he did in his home in June 1830. His congregation was evidently impressed. He "resumed ministerial character" sufficiently to at least be allowed to officiate at weddings.

The settlers also made use of preachers traveling a circuit or just passing through town. Blackman's Tavern, one of the first businesses in the settlement, became a house of worship for the first ordained minister to visit the settlement in mid-August 1830.

It wasn't long, however, before people in the settlement began forming their own congregations and building their own churches. The first organized congregation was the Methodist Episcopal Church, brought together in 1832 under Rev. Elijah H. Pilcher. It was not until 1850, however, that a church building was built and formally dedicated.

Baptists in Jackson built a church, but not without some help. The congregation had trouble getting enough manpower together to raise the frame of the building at Michigan Avenue and Francis Street. Abram Wing, a member of the group, solved the problem by organizing a "raising bee" and making sure to advertise the availability of "plenty of good whiskey."

What became the First Congregational Church in Jackson first organized as a Presbyterian church in 1837. Members of the congregation found they disagreed with the pro-slavery policies of the national Presbyterian Assembly in Philadelphia in 1840.

The majority broke off to organize the Congregational Church. By 1843, the entire former Presbyterian congregation had reorganized as Congregationalists.

The reunited church built a new sanctuary in 1845 and then almost lost it. One of the congregation's pastors preached vigorously in favor of temperance. This apparently incited someone to ignite straw under the pulpit in the empty church. The fire, perhaps providentially, went out on its own with no damage done. In 1860, the Congregationalists completed the church on the north side of the public square that would remain one of downtown Jackson's chief landmarks.

The Greenwood Avenue Methodist Church, organized early in the 20th century, had its start in a saloon. George Dimond, a Michigan Central Railroad employee who had his hand in organizing at least four congregations in Jackson, succeeded in stirring Methodists against a tavern at the intersection of Greenwood Avenue and Fourth Street. The congregation managed to buy the building. However the saloonkeeper, Jacob Nissen, refused to give up his lease. So, for a time, the Methodists held church services on the ground floor while Nissen ran a saloon in the basement.

Other Jackson churches organized included a Catholic church in 1857, the Jackson African Methodist Episcopal Church in 1862, the Second Baptist Church in 1868, the Unitarian Church in 1853, the German Evangelical Lutheran Church in 1864, and the First Free Methodist Church in 1875. The first Jewish synagogue in the city opened in 1863, a year after the Beth Israel congregation organized with five members.

In the 20th century, Grass Lake became the unlikely site of the national headquarters of the Romanian Orthodox Church of America. Jackson County was never a center for Romanian immigration; Romanian Orthodox Church leaders nevertheless purchased W.A. Boland's farm on Grey Tower Road in 1947, making it the official headquarters of the 35,000-member church five years later. The out-of-the-way site did not protect the church from controversy. Church leader Valerian D. Trifa was ordered deported by the U.S. government in 1982. He was accused of being a former leader of the anti-Semitic Iron Guard, a group responsible for killing hundreds in Romania during World War II.

Along with religion, education was nurtured from the very start of Jackson's settlement. Silence D. Blackman, the 26-year-old sister of Horace Blackman, had charge of nine students when the first school opened in 1831. She taught for

Facing page, top: An immersion baptism was a major religious and social event in the 19th century. This one was held circa 1880 in the Grand River, evidently near a church outside of the city. Baptisms were often followed by picnics or additional church services. The first Baptist church in Jackson was built in 1838 at the intersection of Francis Street and Michigan Avenue. Courtesy, Michigan Historical Collections, Bentley Historical Library, University of Michigan (MHC, BHL, UM)

Facing page, bottom: From 1832 to 1969, five successive school buildings occupied the southwest corner of Blackstone Street and Michigan Avenue. This high school served from 1854 to 1879. It was replaced in 1880 by a new high school later known as the William Seaton School. The last school building on the site was the West Intermediate School built in 1918 and torn down to make way for an office building. Courtesy, Jackson District Library

free for the first two years in a log schoolhouse on Jackson Street. Students sat on seats made of split logs. There were no desks. Students held texts, which included the New Testament, on their laps.

In 1832, the people of Jackson voted to build a new schoolhouse on a knoll at the southwest corner of Michigan Avenue and Blackstone Street, a site that would remain used for education for more than a century.

A former student remembered one of the teachers who succeeded Miss Blackman in that "new red school:" "Mr. Adams was quite merciful. He used to whale on the boys occasionally, but I do not remember having seen him whip but one girl and that was for spitting in his face." Of course, life wasn't always easy for teachers. Angry students dragged one teacher out of the schoolhouse and threw him over the bank in front of the school.

For reasons not clear, the Jackson area was carved into two school districts in 1838. Boundaries were a sore spot and often disputed. The illogic of two school districts for one city became apparent, but it wasn't until 1897 that the two districts were joined again with the formation of the Union School District. Even this was over opposition of voters west of the river who voted two-to-one against the merger.

The reuniting of the school districts made possible the building in 1908 of the first public high school serving all students in the city. That building on the northeast corner of Jackson Street and Washington Avenue later became a vocational school and for a time served as city hall.

Land on the west side of Steward Avenue, facing Wildwood Avenue, became the site for the next high school. Jackson High was opened in 1927 along with a stadium named in honor of Phil H. Withington, responsible for donating a major part of the land.

A second public high school, Parkside High, was opened in 1963 on Fourth Street near Ella Sharp Park. But declining enrollment, due to declining birthrates and a movement to the suburbs, forced the closing of many schools in the district. By the fall of 1982, Parkside became a junior high and Jackson, once again, was a one high school district. By 1983, enrollment had dropped to 7,884.

Parochial education in Jackson began in 1857, only months after the completion of St. John Catholic Church. Thanks largely to the influx of Polish Catholics into the community, new parochial schools sprang up with the growth of the Catholic community. The St. Mary parish opened a school in

Facing page, top: *Sarah Blackmore was honored with this card as a "model scholar" at one of the Rives Township schools in 1886. Each township had several school districts, each with its own school, usually one room. Consolidation gradually reduced the number of school districts outside the city to 11, and made the one-room school an institution of the past. Courtesy, Thomas A. Johnson*

Facing page, bottom: *This was the seventh grade class of T.A. Wilson School in 1896. The original school at the intersection of Blackstone and Morrell streets was a two-story brick building called Blackstone School, built in 1887. (MHC, BHL, UM)*

1887, followed by St. Joseph in 1903 and St. Stanislaus in 1920.

Higher education had a fitful start in Jackson County. The Spring Arbor Seminary of the Methodist Episcopal Church was the first college chartered in the county, but before it was really established it moved to Albion where enrollment began in 1840 as the Wesleyan Seminary at Albion. The institution became Albion College.

Spring Arbor had a second chance at a college when in 1844 some Free Will Baptists decided to start a college there. Among the first five students at Michigan Central College were Clinton B. Fisk, who went on to found Fisk University in Nashville, Tennessee, and Livonia E. Benedict, the first woman to be admitted by a Michigan college in a degree program on a par with men. College officials became unhappy with the location, and in 1853 Hillsdale wooed the college away with a promise of $15,000 and a 25-acre campus. The institution became Hillsdale College.

Spring Arbor eventually did have a college. Spring Arbor Seminary opened there in 1873 in the abandoned Michigan Central College buildings. The Free Methodist seminary was, in effect, a private boarding school offering education up through high school level. A college program was begun in 1923 with a two-year junior college program. It was renamed Spring Arbor Seminary and Junior College. The following year, the primary and intermediate departments, which had served mostly children in the Spring Arbor area, were discontinued. The high school continued until 1961 when it, too, was phased out. By that time, the name of the college was changed again, to Spring Arbor College. In May 1965 it became a four-year liberal arts college.

While the campus of Spring Arbor College is the oldest in the county, dating back to its origins as Michigan Central College, the oldest continually operating institution of higher learning in the county is the Jackson Business Institute. George Devlin, a Civil War veteran, began the school as Devlin's Business College in 1867. In nearly 120 years, the institute has had at least six different owners. The site of the school has been moved from building to building in downtown Jackson.

The curriculum has changed, although education in business skills has always been the school's mainstay. In the early days the school offered courses mainly in penmanship and bookkeeping. In the 1880s and 1890s, the school had its own music department. In 1967, the accredited two-year college could offer, in addition to political science, sociology, history, and psychology, a Mr. Executive course for men and a Nancy Taylor

Facing page, top: *This first class of Jackson Junior College sophomores donned hats and coats and stepped outside of Marsh Hall for this picture in the winter of 1929. The school was a year old, with 14 staff members headed by Dean John Paul Jones. Courtesy, Jackson Community College*

Facing page, bottom left: *This Jackson Junior College physics class appears to have been held in Marsh Hall. The college also used classrooms and laboratories at nearby Jackson High. In 1946 classes were held for the first time in John George Hall, also adjacent to the high school. In 1961 the college occupied the West Intermediate building at the intersection of Michigan Avenue and Blackstone Street. Courtesy, Jackson Community College*

Facing page, bottom right: *Marsh Hall was the original building for Jackson Junior College. It stood on Wildwood Avenue west of Jackson High and was named for Edward O. Marsh, Jackson school superintendent from 1911 to 1930. Fire destroyed the 24-room building in 1956. Courtesy,* Jackson Citizen Patriot

Charm Course for women. Both were "aimed at helping the individual perfect the personal traits that contribute toward individual success."

Jackson Community College was a latecomer among Jackson schools. The Union School District established what was called Jackson Junior College in 1928. Its lone campus building was a house adjacent to Jackson High on Wildwood Avenue. The college shared the high school library, gymnasium, laboratories, classrooms, and auditorium. Mainly because of the Great Depression, only 34 of the first 113 who enrolled that first year would graduate. In 1944, at the height of World War II, the school would graduate just 15, all women. The college survived and grew. While it occupied more buildings, it still outgrew its downtown campus. By 1964 the college actually had to turn away qualified applicants.

A donation in 1961 of 270 acres south of the city in Summit Township by Jackson industrialist J. Sterling Wickwire opened new possibilities for the school. After two failures, voters in 1964 approved a millage to build and support the new campus. In 1969 the school, renamed Jackson Community College, was moved to its new campus.

While schools and churches helped define the new community in the wilderness and serve its educational and spiritual needs, they could not provide the sense of unity and civic voice that a newspaper could. So important was a newspaper to the founders of the town that they paid to have one established in the tiny settlement.

The story of news media in Jackson began with a promise from Jackson citizens to Nicholas Sullivan, a 22-year-old printer from Vermont. Prominent Jackson people offered $100 moving expenses and $200 upon arrival to Sullivan to establish a newspaper in Jacksonburg. At the northeast corner of the public square he set up an office and in March 1837 produced the first edition of the *Jacksonburg Sentinel*. It had four pages with five columns per page. A "good stout boy" could print 100 copies per hour on the press which required four impressions to make a single paper. Editorially, the paper soon earned the reputation as a Whig paper.

Other papers followed beginning with the *Michigan Democrat* in 1838, a paper established in response to the *Sentinel* to reflect the Democratic point of view. A temperance paper, an abolitionist paper, and even an anti-Canadian government paper also sprang up, all clearly bent on offering more opinion than news. The anti-Canadian government paper, called *The*

Canadian, was established by Canadian exiles who left Canada during the Patriot War there. Only one edition of *The Canadian* is known to have been published in Jackson, and that in 1839.

None of those early papers survived, but successors did. The *Michigan Democrat* gave way to the *Jackson Patriot* in 1844. This paper, started by Reuben S. Cheney and Wilbur F. Storey, was also strongly Democratic. The *Sentinel* survived until 1840. The *Michigan State Journal* and the *Michigan State Gazette* appeared for a time as an alternative to the *Patriot.* But by 1849 those newspapers had failed, leaving Jackson a one-newspaper town. The Whig sentiment in Jackson did not tolerate that situation for long. Albert A. Dorrance and Charles V. DeLand launched the *American Citizen* in 1849 and with it a long and bitter rivalry between the *Citizen* and the *Patriot.* DeLand accused Cheney, who for a time was also the Jackson postmaster, of not allowing *Citizen* readers to pick up their newspapers at the post office. Cheney, meanwhile, had no qualms about publishing personal attacks against DeLand. One letter to the editor written about DeLand, perhaps by Cheney himself, read: "If monkey grimaces, bar-room brawling, blackguarding and lying, make a man, then I suppose he is one."

The *Jackson Daily Citizen* in 1865 became the first daily paper to last more than a few weeks. By 1889 there were three dailies and seven weeklies in Jackson. One newspaper generously described itself and its rivals:

These dailies and hebdomadals, true to their sacred obligations of their office, "speak the truth, the whole truth, and on a very easy pinch, more than the truth." They guard the liberties of the country, and morality, promote religion, overlook the interests of baseball clubs, learnedly discuss the achievements of the turf — and furnish an excellent medium for advertising.

The year 1905 produced a major change in daily newspaper operations in Jackson. That year, Ralph H. Booth and John George purchased the *Industrial News,* a newspaper with little circulation. They made known their intention of making the *News* the third evening paper in town, along with the *Evening Press* and the *Jackson Citizen.* That was enough to convince James O'Donnell, owner of the *Citizen* to sell out to George and Booth. Now with two papers, George and Booth set out to deal with the owners of the *Morning Patriot* and the *Evening Press.* When the dealing was over, two newspapers emerged: the

Facing page, top left: *Charles V. DeLand, son of pioneer settler William DeLand, was editor of the* American Citizen *and was influential in organizing the 1854 Republican convention in Jackson. He later fought in the Civil War, became a state legislator, and wrote a history of Jackson County. Courtesy, Kenneth J. Wyatt*

Facing page, top right: *Wilbur F. Storey edited the strongly Democratic* Jackson Patriot *in the late 1840s and early 1850s. He went from Jackson to become owner of the* Detroit Free Press *and the* Daily Chicago Times, *which he made into a vigorously Copperhead newspaper opposing the administration during the Civil War. His attacks on President Lincoln were so strong that a Union general ordered the newspaper shut down. Courtesy, Kenneth J. Wyatt*

Facing page, bottom: *James O'Donnell, the man standing on the left side of the open doorway, operated the* Jackson Daily Citizen *from 1865 until he sold out in 1905, about the time this picture was taken. He also served as Jackson mayor and representative in Congress. (MHC, BHL, UM)*

Facing page, top: *This was the newsroom of the* Jackson Citizen Patriot *in 1937, 100 years after the* Jacksonburg Sentinel *made its debut. The* Citizen Patriot *building at the northwest corner of Washington Avenue and Jackson Street was built in 1927. From 1918 to 1927 the paper was printed at the corner of Mechanic and Cortland streets. Courtesy,* Jackson Citizen Patriot

Facing page, bottom left: *Carl M. Saunders, editor of the* Jackson Citizen Patriot *from 1937 to 1961, won a Pulitzer Prize for his 1949 editorial entitled "First Things First," which was a plea to designate Memorial Day as a day to pray for peace. In 1950, largely because of Saunders' efforts and the influence of the editorial, President Truman issued a proclamation calling on Americans to observe Memorial Day. Saunders was also influential in introducing civil service in Michigan. (MHC, BHL, UM)*

Facing page, bottom right: *This 1935 WIBM musical program was probably broadcast from the Otsego Hotel at Michigan Avenue and Francis Street. The station, which first aired as WIBJ, also broadcasted from the Reynolds Building and the Hotel Hayes before moving to studios on Kibby Road in 1947. Jack Paar, host of the "Tonight Show" in the 1950s, worked for the station in the mid-1930s. (MHC, BHL, UM)*

Morning Patriot and the evening *Citizen Press.*

In 1915 the *Citizen Press* became a part of Booth Publishing, a chain of Michigan newspapers begun in 1890 by George Booth, apparently no relation to Ralph Booth. Booth Publishing gained control of the *Patriot* in 1918 and the two papers were combined to become the *Jackson Citizen Patriot.* Rival dailies sprang up — the *Jackson News* in 1918 and the *Jackson Tribune* in 1926. But none survived and since 1936 only one daily, the *Jackson Citizen Patriot,* has served Jackson County.

While the *Jackson Citizen Patriot* emerged as the lone daily newspaper published in the county, it was not without competition. Radio came to Jackson in 1925 with the first locally produced show broadcast from the basement of the Capitol Theater in downtown Jackson. The station, first called WIBJ, later became WIBM, and broadcast from the Reynolds Building, the Otsego Hotel, and the Hayes Hotel before moving in 1947 to new quarters on Kibby Road in Summit Township.

Television came upon the scene in Jackson only after a four-year legal battle before the Federal Communications Commission. Four groups fought for the rights to the Jackson station including both the owners of WIBM and WKHM. There were two winners: Michigan State University and Television Corporation of Michigan, owners of radio station WILS of Lansing. The license to broadcast was the first of its kind. For 38 hours per week channel 10 would be WMSB-TV, broadcast from the campus of Michigan State University in East Lansing. For the other 66 hours per week, channel 10 would be WILX-TV, broadcast out of Jackson. The first part-educational, part-commercial station in the country began programming on March 15, 1959. The arrangement lasted until 1971 when Michigan State University acquired its own separate channel.

By the decade of the 1980s, Jackson's educational, religious, and media institutions were far different from the simple newspapers, schools, and churches begun 150 years earlier. But just like those first institutions they continued to serve the mind, spirit, and voice of the community and like those institutions they would continue to evolve as the character of the community changed.

THE FIRST REPUBLICAN CONVENTION

The issue of slavery gripped the nation in the mid-19th century as no issue has done before or since. While most in Jackson did little, some felt the moral obligation to help fugitive slaves. In Jackson there were at least three agents of the underground railroad, the clandestine system set up by abolitionists to spirit away fugitive slaves from the South through the North and into Canada. Two of the Jackson agents were Lonson Wilcox and Norman Allen. The "station," where fugitives were brought for rest, meals, or hiding on their way through, was a house on the

---

Below: *President Taft paraded through Jackson on June 4, 1910, on his way to dedicate the boulder that marks the birthplace of the Republican Party at Franklin and Second streets. Taft rode in merchant L.H. Field's Pierce-Arrow for the occasion. The Republican monument became a favorite stumping place for Republican politicians through the years. (MHC, BHL, UM)*

southeast corner of Cortland Street and Blackstone Street.

Jackson, however, seems to have been less fervently anti-slavery than many of its Michigan neighbors. People in Kalamazoo and Battle Creek were more active in the underground railroad. People in Grand Rapids actually elected a mayor, Wilder D. Foster, primarily on the issue of checking the spread of slavery to new territories.

Jackson became the focal point of the issue in the state mainly because of its geography and the influence of a few local leaders. It became the birthplace of the Republican Party because it was in Michigan that the ferment of political unrest happening everywhere in the North was first manifested in the form of a new political organization.

The Kansas-Nebraska Bill was the catalyst that made the formation of a new political party inevitable. The bill said that people in new states

would decide for themselves whether slavery would be permitted or banned. Many in the North saw the passage of the Kansas-Nebraska Bill as a great defeat for the North because it gave the South an opportunity to extend slavery into many states and shift the delicate political balance in the nation in favor of the South and slavery sympathizers.

Debate over the pending bill stirred local, state and national leaders of the foundering Whig Party and various minor parties to coalesce. In Michigan, prominent Whig newspaper editors including Charles DeLand of the *Jackson Citizen* met with Free Soil leaders at the state convention of the Free Soil Party at the Marion House in Jackson. Their purpose was to feel out interest in a fusion party. A

Above: *Austin Blair, a participant at the first Republican convention, served as a state legislator, U.S. congressman, and governor. As a legislator he favored removing "white" from the constitution as a qualification for suffrage and was subsequently voted out of office. As governor, he presided over Michigan's war effort and made Jackson the state's military headquarters during the Civil War. Courtesy, Ella Sharp Museum*

Above: *The 100th anniversary of the founding of the Republican Party brought Vice President Richard M. Nixon to Jackson. The July 1954 Freedom Festival was marked by parades, speeches, dances, a beard-growing contest, the selection of a Miss Freedom queen, and a program at the fairgrounds titled "These Truths are Self Evident" with a cast of 1,500. Courtesy,* Jackson Citizen Patriot

subsequent meeting in Kalamazoo produced a call for a state convention on July 6 in Jackson. The appeal for the convention, drawn by a committee including Austin Blair and M.A. McNaughton of Jackson, read:

A great wrong has been perpetrated. The slave power of the country has triumphed. Liberty is trampled underfoot. The Missouri compromise, a solemn compact entered into by our fathers, has been violated, and a vast territory, dedicated to freedom, has been opened to slavery ... We invite all our fellow-citizens, without reference to political associations, who think that the time has arrived for a union at the North to protect liberty from being overthrown and downtrodden, to assemble in MASS

CONVENTION on Thursday, the 6th of July next, at 1 o'clock p.m., AT JACKSON There to take such measure as shall be thought best to concentrate the popular sentiment of this state against the agression of the slave power.

Jackson made a convenient site for a convention because it was the largest town in the central part of the state. It was also home to several influential organizers of the convention. DeLand, in particular, was responsible for much of the behind-the-scenes work in getting the convention organized.

The town prepared several weeks for the convention, its purpose seeming ever more urgent with the formal passing of the Kansas-Nebraska Act on May 22. At least 3,000 and as many as 5,000 came to Jackson.

Bronson Hall was plainly not large enough to accommodate the crowd so the convention adjourned to an oak grove where a platform and temporary seating had been prepared. The area was on the western outskirts of town near what became the intersection of Second Street and Washington Avenue. Wrote a historian on the fiftieth

anniversary of the occasion:
The scene, as the crowd moved toward the grove was an inspiring one. As far back as the eye could reach was a procession of men, with many women, also. The grove itself was a beautiful piece of woods, situated on what was known as "Morgan's Forty," situated between the village and the race course. The scene there was an animated one, suggesting a huge picnic, the Jackson brass band enlivening the occasion with patriotic airs.

The real work of the convention was done nearby in a clump of oaks near what became the intersection of Franklin and Second streets. A 16-member committee was assigned to prepare a platform for the convention. The platform demanded the repeal of the Fugitive Slave Law, which required that fugitive slaves captured in the North be returned to the South. The platform promised that the North would defend non-slaveholders against slaveholders in the territories. And, of course, it called for the repeal of the Kansas-Nebraska Act.

The convention did not call for the abolition of slavery. These people, the majority at least, were not abolitionists. Their main aim was to contain slavery, which they saw as an economic and political threat to the North.

DeLand, writing years later, credited Zephaniah B. Knight, editor of the *Pontiac Gazette*, for coining the name Republican. The convention embraced the name in the following resolution:
That in view of the necessity of battling for the first principles of republican government, and against the schemes of aristocracy the most revolting and oppressive with which the earth was ever cursed, or men debased, we will co-operate and be known as REPUBLICANS until the contest be terminated.

CHAPTER THREE

A Place to Work

Facing page: *The Briscoe was the only automobile produced in Jackson during World War I, as other carmakers turned to the production of shells and airplane parts. This Briscoe assembly line was 500 feet long, shown here circa 1918. (MHC, BHL, UM)*

The health and character of Jackson, as in many communities, has been inextricably tied to its role as a workplace. For Jackson there have been many roles. Jackson has been wagonmaker and wheelmaker; it has been miner of coal and peddler of electricity; it has made corsets and farm hoes, car parts and airplane parts; it has been railroad town, car town and, always, prison town.

Jackson, like most towns formed in the early 19th century, began as a farming community. Even after Jackson became a city, farming was still common for years within the city limits. In 1863, six years after the city was incorporated, farmers harvested 400 bushels of wheat in just one of the four city wards. The county as a whole led the state for a time in the production, packing, and shipping of beans. An 1895 publication boasted that Jackson County grew more corn per acre than anywhere east of the Mississippi River.

The county also earned a reputation for the quality and speed of its horses. In the late 19th century some liked to claim Jackson as the Lexington of the North for its speedy stock of horses, including Tremont, sire of Junemont, reputed to be the fastest five-year-old horse in the world in 1888. Summed up one proud Jackson writer: "Some of the finest roadsters are bred here and he is a fortunate habitue of the turf whose pockets have not been depleted by backing an opinion adverse to the speed of our equine clippers."

But Jackson, from very early on, was more than a farming town. For good or ill, its prison has been its most enduring industry. Jackson people did not always relish the association. To many people in the state Jackson became like Sing Sing or Leavenworth, synonymous with prison. But the prison was important to Jackson's early growth. By providing cheap prison labor, it was probably the biggest factor in Jackson's industrial head start over many Michigan cities.

Tamaracks cut into poles formed the stockade for the prison which accepted its first prisoner — John McIntyre of Wayne County — on January 12, 1839. Even after stone walls were built, beginning in 1841, it was common to refer to someone sentenced to prison as having "gone to the tamaracks."

But neither tamaracks nor stone walls could prevent the

inevitable. Of 35 inmates sent to Jackson the first year, seven managed to escape. In 1841 a "robber gang" of as many as 40 inmates overpowered guards and escaped. Eight to 10 were apparently never caught. Jackson citizens armed themselves and pursued the gang leader all the way to Spring Arbor where, after refusing to surrender, he was shot dead.

There was good reason to escape. The prison was an unforgiving institution. It employed the Auburn system, considered to be progressive for its time. Under the system inmates were made to work both as a form of punishment and regeneration, but also as a way to make the prison self-supporting. The prison also employed the so-called silent system, where inmates weren't allowed to talk with one another. Methods of punishment ranged from flogging, to being shackled in solitary confinement, to being forced to wear an "iron cap," an iron basket strapped to the head.

The prison proved to be a boon to Jackson in the 19th century mainly because of the introduction of contract labor. Under the contract system started in Jackson in 1843, a business could contract with the prison to employ inmates for far less than they could hire free labor. One of the first contracts, employing about 15 inmates in the making of carriages and wagons, paid 33.5 cents per day for each inmate.

Cheap prison labor was employed making furniture, boots and shoes, cigars, horse collars, and many other products. In particular, the labor helped establish Jackson as a center for the manufacture of wagons and agricultural implements.

By the turn of the century, pressure grew to end the contract prison labor system. People viewed it as corrupt and as unfair competition with free labor. In 1909 the state legislature abolished the practice. The prison's last contract, one with the Michigan Seating Company, expired shortly after World War I.

Although the prison no longer provided a manufacturing advantage for the city, it continued as a manufacturer and as a major employer. Instead of making products for private industry, inmates worked on farms and in plants owned and operated by the state. The first prison farm was started in 1909 and a canning factory began operation in 1911. By 1916, state prison factories were producing binder twine, fiber chairs, boxes, brooms and dusters, stone monuments, brick, and tile. Inmates were later employed in making many metal products including automobile license plates and furniture.

While outsiders viewed Jackson as a prison town, it was never entirely dependent on the prison even during the years of the

Facing page, top: Austin, Tomlinson and Webster employed as many as 125 inmates at a rate of 40 cents per day manufacturing the so-called "Jackson Prison Wagon." At its peak in 1889, the company produced 193 wagons. Famous for its flamboyant marketing techniques, the Austin, Tomlinson and Webster Manufacturing Company sent wagons aloft by hot-air balloon and staged competitions against other wagons. Company officials were particularly proud of a letter from the showman P.T. Barnum thanking the company for making a wagon strong enough to carry the elephant Jumbo. Courtesy, Ella Sharp Museum

Facing page, bottom: Jennie Merriman was a trotting horse from the Sharp family's Hillside farm. The horse was shown here circa 1895 at the grounds of the Jackson County Driving Club. (MHC, BHL, UM)

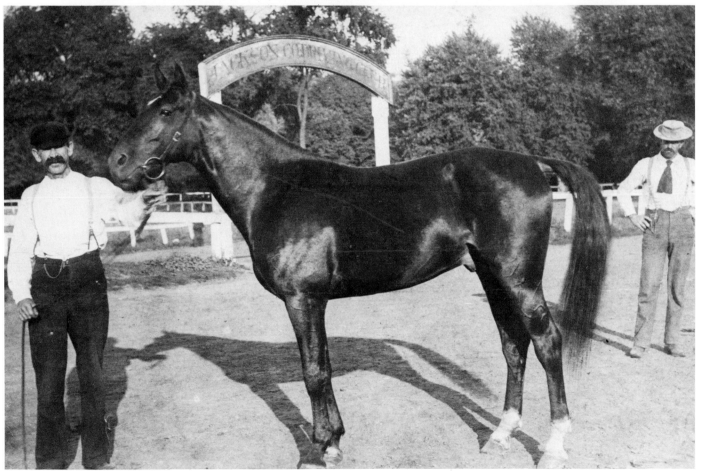

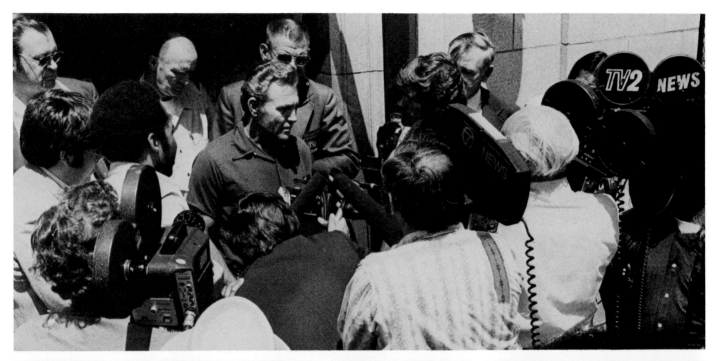

contract system. Many small companies sprang up in the 19th century and thrived, at least briefly. Some employed contract labor; most did not. Jackson was home to several cigar makers, each with its own colorful brand names: Evening Delight, Figaro, Little Ray, White Ash, Central City, and La Flor de Portia. Many were made from tobacco raised west of the city. In 1884 there were at least two breweries: the Haenle Brewing Company and the Jackson Brewing and Malting Company. Jackson companies also made sewer pipe and paving bricks. From 1894 to 1909, the Novelty Manufacturing Company in Jackson produced more than one million small oil heaters and stoves. The company developed the first efficient oil heater with a round wick and exported it to Europe. For a time early in the 20th century, thanks mainly to the Gilbert Candy Company, Jackson gained a national reputation for the making of chocolate creams and nut and fruit candies.

Besides these smaller companies, there emerged in the 19th century three dominant industries. They were coal mining, corset making, and railroading.

The first coal mine in Jackson County, perhaps the first in Michigan, was dug in 1856 along Sandstone Creek, possibly near O'Brien Road in Spring Arbor Township. This 127-foot shaft became the Hayden & Reynolds Mine, the first of at least 47 mines and probably more in the county. Mining never dominated Jackson's economy as it did cities in West Virginia and Kentucky, but in 1873 it was considered Jackson's major industry. In 1880, at the industry's height, miners dug 125,000 tons of the black fuel from beneath Jackson soil. In coal mining's heyday, more than 1,000 people, including prison inmates, were employed in various phases of mining operations.

The mines, clustered within and west of the city, each had names usually far more picturesque than the mines themselves: Black Diamond, New Hope, White Rose, Bonanza, and Shamrock. Coal from Jackson tended to be high in sulphur content and therefore was not as good as coal from out of state. Also, Jackson miners had to contend continually with water that flooded mines. This drove up the cost of digging Jackson coal. As cheaper and better coal could be brought in from Ohio and elsewhere, Jackson mines began to close. By 1902, the industry was all but dead. The coal was still there, however, and there were efforts at reviving the industry. The last attempt was in 1934 when the Grand River Coal Company opened a strip mine in an alfalfa field along Lansing Avenue in Rives Township. That failed after a year, leaving pits and mounds of earth still useless for agriculture nearly 50 years later.

Whereas Jackson's geology gave birth to local coal mining, Jackson's geography was largely responsible for its becoming a center for corset making. Jackson's central position in the Midwest as well as its handy rail connections made the town a good place for the manufacture of corsets and underwear beginning in the 1870s. The local invention of the Bortree Duplex Corset, which became popular, also helped stimulate the concentration of the undergarment industry in Jackson.

Changing fashions and new kinds of elastics made life more comfortable for women after World War I, but they were catastrophes for the city's corset industry. East Coast girdle manufacturers drove most Jackson corset makers out of business. The two that survived after 1934, the Kellogg Corset Company and the S.H. Camp Company, turned to the production of therapeutic or prosthetic support garments and devices.

As with corset manufacturing, Jackson's geography was important in making it a major railroad center. The story of railroading in Jackson began in 1841 with the completion of the Michigan Central Railroad line west to Jackson from Detroit and Ann Arbor. For three years Jackson benefited as the western end of the railroad line through Michigan, but feelings in the community toward the railroad turned bitter with the so-called Great Railroad Conspiracy Trial in 1851. The notorious trial was the outcome of a long-standing feud between farmers across the state and the Michigan Central Railroad. Farmers felt they were not adequately reimbursed for livestock killed by trains. Many, including some in Jackson County, destroyed railroad property and even fired guns at passing trains. When a November 18, 1850, fire destroyed the Detroit railroad freight depot, railroad officials wanted to pin the blame on a group of farmers in Jackson County led by Abel Fitch, a prosperous Michigan Center farmer and politician who at one time served as Leoni Township supervisor. Fifty Jackson County residents, including Fitch, were arrested and taken to Detroit. There Fitch died of dysentery acquired in the squalor of a Detroit jail. Twelve others were eventually convicted. None completed their prison terms; one escaped, one died in prison, and the remainder were eventually pardoned. The trial left great resentment toward the railroad from Jackson people who never believed the Jackson farmers were responsible for the Detroit fire.

Despite the animosity, railroads were too important to any growing community to turn away. In 1858 Jackson welcomed the completion of a branch of the Michigan South Railroad from

Above, left: *The Eberle Brewing Company produced Blue Star Beer. Beginning in 1896, the company developed soft drink flavors under the Eberle name, and soft drinks were its only business during the Prohibition era, from 1919 to 1933. Brewing resumed after Prohibition until 1941. As the Eberle Bottling Company, the company survived until 1964 when it was sold outside the Eberle family. This ad is circa 1900. Courtesy, Jackson District Library*

Above: *The Eberle Brewing Company was called the Jackson Brewing and Malting Company until its name was changed in 1898. Another Jackson brewer was the Haenle Brewing Company. That company, started in 1879, produced beer at a brewery on Cooper Street until Prohibition. Courtesy, Jackson District Library*

Left: *1910 records show that of Jackson's 4,797 wage-earners, nearly 1,000 were women making corsets, lingerie, skirts, and shirts. The Jackson Corset Company, established in 1884 and shown here circa 1910, employed 300 people in 1895 when it was said to be the largest manufacturer of combination corset and waist garments in the U.S. Corset manufacturers were concentrated on Cortland and Pearl streets, and included the makers of such brand names as Bortree, Coronet, Jackson, Reliance, Pandora, Michigan, and M and E. (MHC, BHL, UM)*

Tecumseh. The new branch enhanced Jackson's role as a rail center by making the town the only interior city where two major branches of competing railroads came nearly together. The competition helped Jackson industry in general by lowering freight costs.

By the 1870s Jackson was at the intersection of six different railroad lines including the Grand Valley Railroad, the Airline Railroad, the Jackson, Lansing and Saginaw Railroad and the Fort Wayne, Jackson and Saginaw Railroad. Jackson had more rail passenger traffic than any city in the state and was second only to Detroit in freight shipped.

In 1871, Jackson became more than a rail transportation center. It became a railroad manufacturing center. That year the Michigan Central Railroad, enticed with 30 acres of land previously designated for a park, located its engine manufacturing and repair shops in Jackson. The decision meant employment for 1,000 people and made Jackson the unquestioned rail capital of Michigan.

Jackson's role as the rail center of Michigan was brief, however. The Jackson shops produced their last 10 locomotives in 1904. The Michigan Central shops still employed about 1,500 and an additional 100 workers earned a living at the nine-bay Grand Trunk Railroad roundhouse which had opened about 1900. But by 1910, Detroit, with 10 railroads, a larger population, more manufacturing, and a rail-link with Canada, resumed its preeminence as the state's rail center.

The advent of the diesel locomotive in the 1930s and 1940s, needing less frequent and different kinds of maintenance, made the Jackson shops obsolete and further deteriorated Jackson's role as a rail center. Only about 200 people continued to be employed by the railroad in Jackson. Well before Jackson left railroading behind, however, it became a leader in a different mode of transportation. Jackson's role as a workplace changed dramatically with the invention and popularization of the automobile.

Jackson's success as a carriage maker may have been one of the reasons why Jackson was late entering automobile manufacturing. Even though it was but a small step from making buggies to making cars, carriage companies may have been reluctant to abandon their own well-established industry for an untried one. Wrote the president of a 1909 buggy company long since extinct: "Buggies will always be used and there will always be a demand for them no matter how universal the use of automobiles become, and we consequently

Facing page, top: *M.H. Kerr, a mute artist living in Jackson in 1879, made this pen-and-ink sketch of the scene following the disastrous October 10, 1879, train wreck. Fifteen people were killed in the accident, when a passenger train plowed into a switch engine and some freight cars in the railroad yards on the southeast side of Jackson. The yard master held accountable, Evander T. Colwell, was said to have gone insane years later on an anniversary of that disaster. On October 13, 1893, another train disaster occurred in Jackson. This time an excursion train from Buffalo appeared out of the morning fog and crashed into a second excursion train from Watertown, New York, standing at the Michigan Central Railroad depot. Both trains were traveling to the World's Columbian Exhibition in Chicago. Thirteen died and 30 were injured, all from Pennsylvania and New York. (MHC, BHL, UM)*

Facing page, bottom: *This Michigan Central Railroad crew operated this steam shovel to prepare the way for new track in the late 19th century. The first rails to reach Jackson were made of wood. (MHC, BHL, UM)*

Above, left: *The office staff of the Argo Motor Company stood outside their Hupp Avenue plant for this picture in 1915. (MHC, BHL, UM)*

Above, right: *The original Jaxon, believed pictured in this circa 1902 photo, was powered by steam. It was the original product of the Jackson Automobile Company, which also produced models with internal combustion engines. The company, besides making the Jaxon and the Jackson, produced the Orlo and the Wolverine. The Jaxons were tested on "almost impassable sections of Union Street and West Avenue," and acquired the slogan "Sturdy as Old Hickory." (MHC, BHL, UM)*

Bottom: *Fifteen workers at the Briscoe Motor Company plant at 818 Wildwood Avenue paused for this photograph, probably in 1915. The company built cars at the Wildwood Avenue plant from 1914 to 1916. After reorganizing as the Briscoe Motor Corporation, operations were moved to a new complex at the southeast corner of Leroy and Horton streets. At its peak, the company property covered 30 acres bounded by North, Horton, Ganson, and Willow streets. (MHC, BHL, UM)*

William H. Withington, shown here circa 1870, was both an industrialist and a Civil War hero. He and Elihu Cooley took over a struggling farm implement manufacturer in 1857 and built it into a major Jackson auto parts maker. The Sparks-Withington Company became a defense contractor with World War II, and remained one into the 1980s. The name of the company became Sparton Corporation in 1856. During the Civil War Withington commanded the first Michigan unit to volunteer for duty. The unit, known as the Jackson Greys, fought at the Battle of Bull Run, where Withington was captured. Courtesy, Jackson District Library.

expect continual increase in our business and in the growth of our institution."

In 1902 with the start of the Jackson Automobile Company, car manufacturing began in earnest in Jackson. Byron Carter, a bicycle shop manager, Charles Lewis, a buggy spring and axle maker, and George Matthews, a buggy maker, got together to found the company and produce the Jaxon steam car.

The company also advertised the Duck, a car designed so that the driver sat and steered from the back seat. Back-seat driving apparently didn't catch on, at least not commercially. There is no evidence the Duck was ever actually made or sold. The Jackson Automobile Company, which folded in 1922, was the first, the longest-lasting, and the most successful Jackson carmaker, but it was not the only one. At least 25 automakers made Jackson their home.

Each produced cars with their own special styles and slogans. The Briscoe was "the car with the half-million dollar motor" and a "French car at an American price." The Imperial had such a bright finish that it "would almost shine in the dark." The Standard Electric was "the car that excells, the car that outsells."

The slogans couldn't help Jackson keep pace with Detroit in automaking. Jackson could not provide the large amounts of money needed for companies to expand with the assembly line-produced, low-cost carmakers from Detroit. After World War I, Jackson carmakers dwindled away. After 1922, the Earl, produced by the Earl Motor Company, was the only car made in Jackson. That company succumbed in 1924.

The death of so many automaking companies was actually not so painful to Jackson as it might seem. In fact, those automakers paved the way for Jackson's more natural role as an automobile parts maker. Jackson couldn't compete with Detroit and Flint, but it could serve those automaking cities. In 1910 there were already four Jackson auto parts makers: Frost Gear and Machine Company, Hayes Wheel Company, American Top Company, and the Lockwood-Ash Motor Company. Lockwood-Ash also produced marine engines. By 1917, Jackson's reputation as an auto parts town was established. By the mid-1920s nearly half of the community's work force was employed in making car parts. Radiators, radiator fans, mufflers, crankshafts, horns, gears, axles, cushions, and springs all at one time or another were made in Jackson.

Of course, automobile manufacturing was not the only industry to grow up in the 20th century. Aviation and electric utilities also came of age. Jackson was shaped by that growth as it became home to Aeroquip Corporation, Consumers Power Company, and Commonwealth Associates.

Aeroquip was the brainchild of Peter F. Hurst, a German-born engineer and student of aviation. Hurst, a 29-year-old employee of a Berlin company, came to New York City in 1939 just one week before the outbreak of World War II. He was supposed to negotiate licensing agreements with American hose-line manufacturers. The young man had gained fame within the German aircraft industry for developing a new aircraft wheel with a disc-type brake. The development of the new wheel led to the perfection of new hose lines for brake fluid. American companies, however, were not interested in making the new kind of hoses. Hurst established a new company.

While visiting Hayes Industries in Jackson, Hurst met with a group of businessmen interested in his plans. With $10,000 to start up the new firm, they convinced Hurst to open Aeroquip in Jackson. As war spread in Europe and Aeroquip's relationship to the German company grew awkward, Aeroquip bought the patent rights and became independent.

The company struggled until the United States entered World War II when, almost overnight, Aeroquip became a vital war plant. Ironically, Hurst, still a German citizen, was officially labeled an "alien enemy" and was not allowed in his own factory after Pearl Harbor.

Aeroquip expanded into other industries after World War II and beginning in 1953 acquired plants and companies in Ohio, California, and Illinois. In 1968 it merged with the Libbey-Owens-Ford Company, a manufacturer of glass products based in Toledo, Ohio. Aeroquip remained a large employer in Jackson, employing 1,104 in the Jackson area in 1983.

Whereas Jackson's auto industry traced its beginnings to buggy manufacturing, Jackson's utility industry sprang from the milling trade. William A. Foote actually wasn't a successful miller. Born and raised in Adrian, he managed to start a mill in the 1880s, where he experimented with rollers made of stone instead of steel. They didn't work very well and Foote was grateful when some people asked his permission to install an electric generator in his mill for some street lights. He became fascinated with that generator and began to dream of the possibilities for the barely-understood phenomenon of electricity.

In 1886, he and his brother, James B. Foote, came to Jackson and convinced the city council to allow them to demonstrate their "dishpan" street lights — carbon points beneath tin

Facing page, top: The Marion-Handley, as well as the Buick and several other cars, were produced at this plant on the southwest corner of Ganson and Wisner streets. It later became a Kelsey-Hayes Company plant. (MHC, BHL, UM)

Facing page, bottom: The Earl automobile featured a reversible front seat to make for easier conversation while motoring. Clarence Earl came to Jackson from Toledo in 1920 and reorganized the Briscoe Motor Corporation the following year into Earl Motors, Inc. The reversible seat didn't catch on but over 10,000 Earls were produced before manufacturing ended in 1924. (MHC, BHL, UM)

Above: *Peter F. Hurst, a German native, came to the U.S. just before the outbreak of World War II. With the help of Jackson businessmen he started Aeroquip Corporation. Hurst died in 1969. Courtesy, Aeroquip Corporation*

Facing page, top: *A Consumers Power Company electric line crew stood next to a service truck for this picture in the 1920s. Through the years the utility has suffered cash shortages from time to time. A company money-squeeze in 1921 led some overenthusiastic construction crews to pilfer telephone company poles. Courtesy, Consumers Power Company*

Facing page, bottom: *Rescuers worked into the night to find trapped workmen following the collapse of the Consumers Power Company building on October 3, 1956. Ten men were killed in the disaster at the building site on Parnall Road in Blackman Township, when the southeast third of the partially completed building gave way. Floors pancaked together and fell into the basement, trapping workmen. A committee appointed by Gov. G. Mennen Williams to investigate the tragedy issued a report vaguely blaming "human error" for the collapse. Courtesy, Jackson Citizen Patriot*

reflectors. The city already had two struggling electric companies providing lighting for downtown stores, but Foote's demonstration won the brothers the right to put up the street lights.

Though the business grew beyond Jackson, it was still on shaky footing until 1899. That year Foote completed the Trowbridge Dam on the Kalamazoo River and successfully transmitted power to Kalamazoo more than 20 miles away. It was a big step for the power business and by 1907 Foote's Commonwealth Power Company, headquartered in Jackson, had effective control of the electric business in five major Michigan cities: Jackson, Albion, Battle Creek, Kalamazoo, and Grand Rapids.

Further consolidation of Michigan utilities produced the Consumers Power Company in 1910. The company grew to be the largest utility in Michigan, serving gas and electric customers throughout most of Michigan's lower peninsula outside of the Detroit area. In 1983 the company employed more than 12,000 people, 4,000 of whom worked in the Jackson area.

Commonwealth Associates was the engineering arm of Consumers Power until 1949. It was born out of the government-ordered breakup of the Commonwealth and Southern Holding Company, the company that owned Consumers Power and other utilities. Commonwealth became a part of Gilbert Associates of Reading, Pennsylvania, in 1973 but remained a large Jackson employer. Employment of 2,100 in 1979 had shrunk to 1,200 by early 1983.

Jackson played many roles as a workplace in its first 150 years and by the beginning of the 1980s seemed due for yet another. The prison was still a significant employer, but people in Jackson were weary of the label "prison town." While Jackson remained an important automobile parts manufacturing center, the significance of that industry appeared to be on the wane and few in Jackson were eager to tie Jackson's fate so closely again to the capricious automobile industry. The utility industry would remain important to Jackson with Consumers Power Company and Commonwealth Associates, but even the promise of those industries carried a shadow in the early 1980s as state and national doubts about nuclear power cut deeply into prospects for both companies. Jackson, indeed, was looking for a new task as a workplace, and that seemed yet beyond the horizon.

CHAPTER FOUR

A Place to Live

While Jackson came to life as a workplace, life came to Jackson in the form of theater, music, literary societies, parks, resorts, and athletic organizations.

Little is known about how early settlers entertained themselves. Temperance lectures from the pulpit, cited in local histories, indicate that many spent their free time either at a saloon, a church, or both.

Because farming was so important in the early years, agricultural competitions were a big event in the town. The first county fair in 1853 featured cattle, hogs, horses, and sheep on display at the village square. The nearby courthouse served as an exhibit hall for displays of fruit, grain, vegetables, and homemade goods. The next year the fair featured a plowing contest, and county and state fairs kept on growing, with Jackson hosting nine state fairs, the last in 1888.

Along with fairs, circuses came to Jackson. As early as 1852, circuses set up tents in a field near what became the intersection of Fourth and Franklin streets. There Jackson people could, in 1883, take their children to see Jumbo, the "largest elephant in captivity," at the Barnum and London United Monster Show. In 1896, Buffalo Bill's Wild West show attracted 10,000 for an afternoon performance.

Indoor theater probably began with the building of the Odd Fellows Hall, sometime in the late 1830s or early 1840s. Built by Benjamin Porter, the first prison warden, the hall stood on the south side of Main Street at Jackson Street and was the first public hall in the village.

The showplace for theater in Jackson in the 19th century was the Hibbard Opera House. The theater, on the southeast corner of Francis and Cortland streets, opened August 25, 1882, with "The Merchant of Venice" starring Edwin Booth, brother of John Wilkes Booth. The theater lasted only 15 years, but it linked the end of one entertainment era with the dawn of a new one. Its final production, hours before it burned in 1897, was a matinee featuring a few vaudeville acts and some projected pictures using a new "cinemagrascope."

Lecturers, traveling stage shows, freak shows, musical groups, often passing on a scheduled tour through southern Michigan, all made their appearances at these 19th century halls.

Ralph Waldo Emerson was one early lecturer, speaking in Jackson in 1854 and 1863. He was an honored guest in the culturally-starved community. He wrote of his first visit through Michigan: "I was made much of as the only man of the pen within five hundred miles, and by rarity worth more than venison or quail."

In 1866 Jackson citizens heard the great showman P.T. Barnum give a lecture on the "art of making money, or success in life." In 1871, 50 cents could buy admission to hear the famed author Samuel Clemens, better known as Mark Twain, give a talk at Union Hall. Clemens was paid $125 for his 75-minute lecture.

Jackson entertainment ranged from the great to the near-great to the bizarre. Jackson people could see Mary Anderson, considered the greatest "Juliet" the world had ever seen; they could hear a man who claimed to be "the only survivor of the Custer Massacre;" or they could witness Barney Baldwin, "the broken-neck wonder," a man with a fractured neck who, when a brace was removed, could peek under his own arm.

A visitor to Jackson in April 1879 could have chosen from this selection: a lecture reviewing Darwin, entitled "Are We Men or Monkeys?," the comic opera "H.M.S Pinafore," and the staging of "Sprague's Original Georgia Minstrels," featuring "20 colored stars and 10 great comedians."

Societies and organizations sprang up, from the Young Men's Association, which established the town's first lending library in 1865, to fraternal and labor organizations, such as the Improved Order of Red Men, the Ancient Order of United Workmen, and the Order of Chosen Friends.

Women could choose from among 20 literary clubs. The *Daily Citizen* proudly noted that the benefit of these groups "is attested by the fact that Jackson women are admired throughout the state for their rare literary attainments and cultural manner."

In addition to such clubs, political reform groups, as diverse as the Ku Klux Klan and the Women's Christian Temperance Union, attracted members in Jackson. The KKK wielded slight influence, but by 1924 it was powerful enough to host a statewide parade and rally in Jackson, attracting over 60,000 participants.

The WCTU was a much stronger influence, particularly as Jackson's growing railroad industry contributed to its reputation as "Little Chicago." Drunkenness was a pervasive problem; 1879 records indicate that of 49 people lodged in the city jail, 34

Facing page: *The ladies of the Mosaic Club gathered in their finery for this picture in the early 1890s. Organized about 1885, the club was one of many women's groups formed in the late 19th and early 20th centuries. Others included the Athena Club, to educate people about elections, and the Town Improvement Society, whose projects ranged from placing anti-spitting cards on streetcars, to "Americanization work" for Polish immigrants, to campaigns against houseflies. Ella Sharp, standing front left, was a member of all three groups. (MHC, BHL, UM)*

Below: *As president of the Town Improvement Society, Ella Sharp's accomplishments included securing a public nurse for the community, maintaining a flower bed at the intersection of Greenwood Avenue and First Street, and furnishing rooms for young women at the YWCA. She had no children herself but was interested in child labor reform and promoting kindergartens. Courtesy, Ella Sharp Museum*

Facing page, top: *Louis and Edward Boos, on either side of the bass drum, reorganized the Central City Cornet and Reed Band in 1876, changing its name to the Boos' First Infantry Band and making it a prominent Jackson musical institution for more than 40 years. Musical groups have been popular with both men and women since 1842, when blacksmith Albert Foster led the first brass band. Other groups included Harmonie, the Franz Shubert Club, and the Seven Octave Club, whose lasting triumph seems to have been a performance featuring five pianos played simultaneously. Courtesy, Stuart Babcock Collection*

Facing page, bottom: *In 1916 the Mandolin Club was one of many musical groups in the city. The 1915-1916 city directory listed no less than four city orchestras: Blake's Orchestra, Boos' Orchestra, Buttelman's Concert Orchestra, and Weed's Orchestra. There was also a chapter of the American Guild of Banjoists, Mandolinists, and Guitarists. (MHC, BHL, UM)*

were charged with drunkenness.

In March 1874, about 400 Jackson women met in the Jackson Christian Church on Francis Street to report on their mission against saloonkeepers. Said one woman: "We might just as well have been engaged in making pie crusts. It probably would have been just as lasting as the saloonkeepers' promises." Later that same month, six of the women sat in protest in a saloon for six hours "without effective results," according to the *Daily Citizen*.

Women heard great WCTU leaders rail, not only against drunkenness, but in favor of increasing women's public role. Said WCTU speaker C.E. Cleveland to a Jackson audience: "It has been proved that the strength, care and thought expended by the average housewife in coaxing a weak-chested, hollow-backed, consumptive geranium two inches would lift a ton three-quarters of a mile and raise $1,000 mortgages out of sight."

Jackson produced its own WCTU leaders in Lucy A. Thurman, a black woman who lectured around the nation and Great Britain, and Mary Torrens Lathrap, president of the Michigan WCTU for 13 years.

Jackson's tradition of civic organizations persisted into the 1970s, when a list of local clubs included the Altrusa Club, Exchange, Civitan Club, Hi-Twelve, Jackson Business and Professional Women's Club, Negro Business and Professional Women's Club, Optimist, Rotary, and Zonta.

While politics and the arts flourished, interest in athletics grew more slowly in Jackson. It began with assorted athletic contests staged from time to time. These could include horse racing, horseshoeing, or just walking. Walking contests seem to have been particularly popular just after the Civil War. One 10-hour "go-as-you-please" race at Union Hall drew a crowd of spectators and a musical send-off by the Central City Band. It also drew seven participants garbed in tights and fancy breeches for the contest to walk around and around the inside of the hall. The winner paced out over 57 miles.

Amateur baseball teams such as the Jackson Mutuals and Casey's Shamrocks drew a following in the 1870s. Even professionals played from time to time in Jackson. In 1888, Jackson had a team in the Tri-state Baseball League which included teams from Kalamazoo, Wheeling, West Virginia, and seven Ohio cities. The "Central City Boys" were guided by an opera house manager and played on a field complete with bleachers, grandstands, and fencing at Fourth and Franklin streets. General admission was 25 cents, bleacher seats 10 cents.

Right: *Willard G. Bailey, the subject of the song "Won't You Come Home Bill Bailey?", was a member of several Jackson music groups, including this string band. His main occupation was music teacher but the 1908 directory also listed him as a seller of "Edison Phonographs and Records, Musical Instruments, and Pyrographic Supplies." His wife, born Sarah Siegrist in Waterloo Township, didn't like the song that made them famous. Courtesy, Stuart Babcock Collection*

Below, right: *Hughie Cannon, left, shown here with collaborator Bill Queen, brought ragtime to Jackson at Diedrich's Saloon on Main Street at the turn of the century. Cannon wrote "Won't You Come Home Bill Bailey?", for his friend Willard G. Bailey. Cannon sold the song to a publisher for $350. The song brought him fame but no fortune, and he drank himself to death at age 39. Courtesy, Jackson Citizen Patriot*

The May 11 opener against Columbus drew 1,502, standing room only. Jackson lost and the league went downhill from there. By September the team ran out of money. The players finished the season, losing twice as many games as they won, and disbanded.

The new century brought new attitudes, new inventions and new ways of living that altered the way Jackson citizens pursued happiness. The growth of the city and improvements in transportation led to the development of parks. Growth created a need for parks and new ways of travel provided ways to get to those open spaces.

Parks were all but neglected in the 19th century in favor of an all-consuming interest in commerce and industry. Village planners had set aside all four corners of the town's main intersection for public use. Seeing commercial value in the property, village fathers began selling that property beginning in 1852.

By 1900, just about the only parks in Jackson were the fairgrounds, Blackman Park, and .6-acre Greenwood Park at Greenwood Avenue and Jackson Street. A gift to the city in 1836 from pioneer William J. Moody, Greenwood Park was the city's first park. In 1984 the tiny park was renamed Governor Austin Blair Memorial Park.

Loomis Park became the city's first large neighborhood park in 1902. Ten years later, Julia C. Withington, widow of William H. Withington, Civil War general and Jackson industrialist, gave to the city Withington Park, a small triangular piece of land at Michigan and Wildwood avenues.

That gift was dwarfed by a gift that same year from another Jackson woman. Ella Wing Merriman Sharp, widow of one-time state senator John Sharp, died in 1912. She left to Jackson her 530-acre family farm with its farmhouse and outbuildings southwest of the city in Summit Township. Overnight Jackson was overwhelmed with parkland. It was three years before development of the park began and 14 years before the development was completed with ballfields, a golf course, and a rose garden.

Eventually more facilities were added. A zoo was introduced around 1932 and included its own raccoon cage, monkey hill, buffalo den, an elephant named Mary, and a bear named Susie. The zoo fell into disrepair and was dismantled about 1953. The Victorian home became the Ella Sharp Museum in 1965. Peter F. Hurst Planetarium was added to the complex in 1969.

Just as the development of Ella Sharp Park was completed in the late 1920s, Jackson gained another park almost as large. This

Facing page, top: *The hotel at Eagle Point on Clark Lake was a popular getaway in 1910 when this picture was taken. A dance pavilion built on Eagle Point in 1922 featured as many as three bands on a single weekend. (MHC, BHL, UM)*

Facing page, center: *Employees of the Capitol Theater gathered for an outing and a photograph at Pleasant Lake in 1928. The theater where they worked began as the Orpheum in 1916, and was torn down in 1975. (MHC, BHL, UM)*

Facing page, bottom: *The Hague Park flyer was a popular ride at the amusement park at Vandercook Lake. A fire in 1923 destroyed much of the park, which was then renamed Lakeview Park in 1926. Courtesy, Max Brail*

was a gift of William Sparks, a man who served three terms as mayor, dominated Jackson politics and business in the early 20th century, and left his mark in many areas of Jackson life.

Sparks' lasting monument to posterity was William and Mathilda Sparks Foundation County Park, known by most Jackson people as Cascades Park. The 465-acre park, partly in the city and partly in Summit Township, was created in 1929 and dominated by a man-made waterfall built under Sparks' guidance. The Cascades were modeled after a similar waterfall in Havana, Cuba, and inspired by fountains and waterways in Italy, France, and Spain. Sparks stipulated that only Jackson labor be used in building the falls and that married men be given preference in hiring. Some of Sparks' plans for the falls were never realized. He had envisioned a tower at the top of the 75-foot hill from which the falls descended. He also intended to have a prado, a paved walkway extending from the base of the falls 2,100 feet to Griswold Street. The falls nevertheless were a grand achievement. The Cascades included 11 waterfalls, three pools, and six fountains all illuminated with colored electric lights, becoming a regional attraction after opening in 1932.

Almost simultaneous with the growth of public parks in the county came the development of resorts and amusement parks. With some 700 lakes and plenty of undeveloped area, the county had long been an inviting place for boating, picnicking, hunting, and fishing. As early as 1855, Wolf Lake, south of Grass Lake, was a popular resort area. The development of better transportation, particularly trolleys, breathed new life into these resort areas. In fact, trolley companies often helped develop the resorts in order to boost the use of trolleys on weekends and holidays. At Wolf Lake a trolley route opened about 1902, bringing customers every hour, and as many as 3,000 per day from the city.

Improved transportation also helped produce Hague Park, an amusement park at Vandercook Lake. Edrick Hague bought the land and developed it for picnicking and bathing before 1900. It became an amusement park after 1907 when three so-called "Pittsburgh Millionaires" led by James A. O'Dell acquired it. Over the years the park included a vaudeville house, a dance hall, and various rides including the Jack Rabbit roller coaster. Packed trolleys from the city brought crowds as large as 40,000 on Fourth of July weekends.

As the use of the trolley declined, so did the park. It was sold and renamed Lakeview Park in 1926 but was abandoned and sold bit by bit after the Great Depression. What was left of it became Vandercook Lake County Park in 1938, two years after the last trolley ran in Jackson. In 1983, the park was renamed Townsend F. Beaman County Park after a local patent attorney who long had a special interest in the park.

Golf was introduced about 1898. That year Clara Carter Waldron rounded up 30 interested novices and laid out the county's first golf course at Wisner and Ganson streets. The nine-hole course became the Old Meadow Heights Club. The course was abandoned in 1926, but it sparked an interest in the sport. An 18-hole course opened at Ella Sharp Park in 1923. Another course opened at Sparks Foundation County Park in 1932. By 1970, Jackson County had more golf courses per capita than all but a handful of metropolitan areas in the country.

Basketball became an attraction in the new century. As with baseball, Jackson had its own short-lived professional team. The Consumers Power Red Devils, a mix of professional players and former college stars, played from 1926 to about 1929 in the National Professional Basketball League. Their home court was an auditorium at the fairgrounds. The Red Devils played teams from Chicago, Philadelphia, and Cleveland and even went up against the original Celtics from New York, considered the best basketball team of the era.

Later on, harness racing was re-established as a Jackson sport. Jackson, long associated with horses because of the high quality of the stock bred in the county in the 19th century, was a natural area for horse racing. The Jackson Horse-Breeders Association in 1872 built a track and held races at the fairgrounds. On the first day of racing the association offered 10 purses totalling $12,000. They admitted ladies to the track free, "a step which," supporters said, "gave character and tone to the enterprise."

Whatever its character and tone, regularly scheduled racing apparently lost favor late in the century and was discontinued. There were still special races in the area, some on frozen lakes. A 1916 race between Lady Wilberforce of Albion and Jessie G. of Detroit drew 1,200 spectators out onto the ice at Vandercook Lake.

Regular racing resumed at the fairgrounds in 1948 with the establishment of the Jackson Trotting Association. Leon A. Slavin, a businessman associated with the paper industry in Kalamazoo, almost single-handedly kept the association going, taking over as president in 1949. After Slavin's death in 1974, his daughter Nanette Slavin took over operation of the pari-mutuel track.

As the 20th century brought new demands for parks, it also brought changing demands in theater. Vaudeville and motion pictures gave Jackson new kinds of entertainment and altered the town's theater life. The Athenaeum, which also served as a public library and eventually housed the Jackson Business Institute, was one of the first vaudeville and motion picture theaters. It opened in 1898 as a legitimate theater. Said a Jackson *Saturday Evening Star* review:

The majority of plays offered are inconsequential if harmless. They are intended ... to cater to the passing fancy of an overworked people who by constant association, begin to look upon classic plays as ... a bore .... For the good of the stage once in a while a great player comes along, and the low sluggish brain tissues are expanded, grand emotions stirred, tremendous enthusiasms awakened.

Among the stars of the day to awaken sluggish Jackson brains were Ethel Barrymore and Lillian Russell, who both appeared at the Athenaeum in 1907.

Vaudeville came to the Athenaeum by 1910. That year Al Jolson appeared at the theater. Vaudeville productions typically included a four-piece orchestra, a short, silent news reel, and several comedy and singing acts. In 1915, the Athenaeum became the Majestic.

One early vaudeville theater was the Capitol Theater which opened in 1916 as the Orpheum. The Orpheum was a grand showplace. Its innovative asbestos curtain reproduced a scene from the Vatican garden, of the Pharoah's daughter finding the infant Moses in the bulrushes. Three kinds of marble were used for the entrance. The drinking fountains were marble and walnut. Its proscenium arch and organ loft were colored ivory and gold. The nine dressing rooms under the stage were equipped with electric circuits for the chorus girls' curling irons.

At the Orpheum and the Bijou at Francis and Cortland streets, Jackson audiences had a chance to see some of the great stars of the day. Seventeen-year-old Fred Astaire and sister Adele danced at the Orpheum. Jack Benny played violin at the Orpheum. Audiences saw Will Rogers perform rope tricks and Bill Robinson tap dance. Appearing in 1913 was the comedy team of four brothers in an act called "Mr. Green's Reception." They were greeted by the "largest and most pleased audiences" of the season, according to the *Citizen Press*. Ran the newspaper review of the brothers Julius, Leonard, Arthur, and Milton: "Of the four Marx brothers it is impossible to say too much in praise."

The first moving picture of any sort shown in Jackson was probably a film of the Corbet-Sullivan fight screened at Assembly Hall a few weeks or months after the September 7, 1892, bout. The motion picture "The Great Train Robbery" was shown in a tent in a coal yard in 1903 or 1904.

Movie theaters came later, beginning in 1906 with the Subway Theater at 210 E. Michigan and the Star Theater at 107 W. Michigan. Later theaters included the Temple, the Victor, the Rialto, the Wonderland, the Strand, the Colonial, and the Family. With the coming of television, the theaters gradually died out. Only three remained in 1961 and 19 years later only one remained. By then, it too had stopped showing regular movies and its future was in doubt.

There was still theater, but it was no longer downtown. There were two drive-ins on the outskirts of town as well as movie theaters at each of the two major malls: Paka Plaza and Westwood Mall. For stage performances, the community was served primarily by the three theaters at the George E. Potter Center at Jackson Community College.

Jackson nurtured music and theater. The Wright Players were a well-known stock company that performed in Ohio and Michigan. The group first appeared in Jackson in 1926 and performed at the Majestic. During one period the company performed a solid run of 92 weeks, the longest in the United States at the time. The Little Theater Guild of Jackson staged its first play in 1929 at the Majestic. The group eventually became the Jackson Civic Theater. The Clark Lake Players first appeared in 1954 as the Jackson Players Club at the Pleasant View Hotel Dance Pavillion. In 1965, Jackson Community College became home to the Rosier Players, an old-time dramatic theatrical company that traced its beginnings to 1898. In 1944 the Jackson Federation Concert Orchestra was organized. It didn't last, but its descendant, the Jackson Symphony Orchestra, did, organized in 1951.

Jackson of the 1980s was a distant place from the culturally starved community of more than a century earlier. By comparison with some of its larger neighbors there was still much lacking in terms of artistic and cultural life, but Jackson people were proud of what they had: a new community college theater complex and a county rich in lakes, parks, and recreational facilities. The people who came to Jackson came mainly because they saw the town as a good place to work. They stayed because it was a good place to live.

Facing page, top: *The development of Ella Sharp Park and its rose garden led to the creation of the Rose Festival. Initially undertaken as a way to help sell camera film, the Rose Festival grew from a modest parade and rose show in 1958 to a weekend of more than a dozen activities involving thousands of people. By the early 1980s the festival included not only a parade attracting more than 150 entrees, but a softball tournament, a mile run, chicken barbecues, a square dance, a Mr. Rose City Physique Contest, and a contest for Rosequeen. Courtesy,* Jackson Citizen Patriot

Facing page, bottom: *A rock festival at Goose Lake Park in 1970, featuring Alice Cooper, Bob Seger, the James Gang, and Chicago embroiled Jackson in controversy. Residents, property owners, Leoni Township, and Jackson County all went to court to block the concert, which was billed by promoter Richard Songer as "three days of heavy sounds, combined with swimming, parking, camping, picnicking and amusements." As many as 300,000 people attended the peaceful festival, tying up traffic and keeping police busy with drug arrests. Songer was indicted for selling narcotics at the festival, and found not guilty. Calling the event an outrage, Gov. William G. Milliken joined local officials in preventing further rock festivals at Goose Lake. Courtesy,* Jackson Citizen Patriot

CHAPTER FIVE

The Changing Community

Facing page: *Jackson became the first community in Michigan outside of Detroit to have telephone service, with its first subscribers in 1879. Said a Michigan Bell manager: "At times it was almost as easy to open the window and shout to your party as it was to talk to him over the telephone." Telephone installers and repairmen are shown here in about 1895, poised for a day's work, in front of their red brick offices on Cortland Street. The building survived into the 1980s as the Knights of Columbus building. (MHC, BHL, UM)*

Looking back more than 150 years to Jackson's founding, it's difficult to imagine the excitement and uncertainty that early settlers experienced upon arriving at the hamlet on the Grand River. In a letter to her family in Connecticut, Lucy Stowe Morgan, wife of Elijah William Morgan, gave some sense of life in Jacksonburg in 1831 when the settlement was barely two years old:

There are now about 20 houses in the village and three stores. But a good many houses are building this summer and I should think by next spring there should be 30 to 40. It is a year last May since the first house was built and the whole county is settling very rapidly. You cannot have an idea of the tide of emigration that is flowing into Michigan. There is a constant stream of moving going on to the west and many who have improved their farms some sell them at a small advance that they may go west and buy more land at the government price.

Even some of the founders of the town didn't stay around to see what they had wrought. Horace Blackman stayed just six years before buying a farm near Pleasant Lake in Rives Township and moving there. His brother Russell sold his Jackson property in 1845 and joined a Mormon settlement in Illinois.

For those who stayed, life could be lonely and uncertain. Mrs. Morgan lamented in her letter her fear of not living long enough to see Connecticut again. She complained that there was no seafood and little fresh fruit and that Jacksonburg "is like almost all places that grow up suddenly, not distinguished for morality." She added that there is also great opportunity for wealth. "A farmer may grow rich as fast as he pleases."

Growth stopped after the initial surge of settlement. This was partly due to the loss of important community leaders, including Lemuel Blackman, who died in 1835, and I.W. Bennett, who moved to Union City. Also, settlers traveling west began using the Chicago Road to the south, thus bypassing Jackson County. By 1837, according to one source, there were still only 26 structures in the settlement.

Aided by the construction of the railroad to Jackson and by the decision of the state to locate the prison in the community, Jackson enjoyed steady growth after 1837. By 1850, the town had 686 buildings and 3,109 people. Reported the *Jackson Citizen* in 1853:

... building is all the rage here now. There never was a time when there was so many new houses and buildings being erected. Our merchants and mechanics are all busy, busy, busy. Lumber and all kinds of materials are scarce and high. Of personal knowledge, we can count twenty new buildings in course of erection. What town can beat this?

Growth brought the need for more effective government. The Village of Jackson was incorporated in 1843. The original village boundaries encompassed 1,440 acres. But for reasons now unclear, village boundaries were reduced in 1844 to 880 acres bounded by Fourth Street on the west, Ganson Street on the north, Ellery and Johnson streets on the east, and Morrell Street on the south. A.V. Berry was the first president of the village council, which included six trustees assisted by a recorder, treasurer, marshal, street committee, attorney, and two assessors.

In 1857, Jackson became a city and J.C. Wood its first mayor. Its system of government was known as the aldermanic system. Aldermen were elected from the four city wards to a council presided over by the mayor, elected at large. The mayor had veto power over the council.

The earliest settlers were mainly from New York and New England. Few were wealthy, but they tended to be relatively well educated; some were professionals, and many were at least rich enough or had credit enough to buy land or start businesses.

Before long they were joined by others with far different backgrounds. The Irish were probably the first immigrant group to arrive in Jackson in any significant number. About 20 families arrived in the late 1830s or early 1840s to help build the prison. They formed the core of the Catholic community. More Irish came in the 1860s in the huge wave of Irish immigration caused by the Great Potato Famine in Ireland.

In the 1860s, Germans came in large numbers to America because of revolution and war in their homeland. Many found their way to Jackson, where a labor shortage during the Civil War gave them plenty of opportunity for work. Many Jews and Lutherans came with this wave of immigrants. The Jews, many of whom lived in the area near Francis and Euclid streets, were

Facing page, top: *The Guscinski grocery store was one of the businesses that lined Page Avenue and served nearby Polish neighborhoods in the early 20th century. This building survived into the 1980s as the B.W. Bartus Insurance Agency. Courtesy, Frank Machnik Collection*

Facing page, bottom: *Living along Lake Street on Jackson's east side early in the 20th century meant living close to railroad tracks and smokestacks and along a dirt street. It also meant ice delivery by horse-drawn wagon. Courtesy, Frank Machnik Collection*

mainly merchants. Others from Germany worked as carpenters, shoemakers, tailors, potters, butchers, brewers, clerks, blacksmiths, and cigarmakers.

Many of the new Jackson citizens, attracted to the city by opportunities at railroad yards and coal mines, were Poles. Polish immigration began in the 1870s as Polish-speaking Europeans escaped the Russo-Turkish War. Early Polish immigrants lived in an area between North Street and Hill Street, west of Myrtle Street and east of Lansing Avenue. Settlement spread to a neighborhood southwest of Monroe and Blackstone streets. Polish neighborhoods on the east side of Jackson developed after 1904 with the establishment of St. Joseph Catholic Church at Waterloo and Leroy streets. By 1910, Polish-speaking people became the third largest foreign-born group in the city behind Germans and Canadians. By then there was a diverse blend of immigrants in the community, including Austrians, Italians, Greeks, Swedes, Belgians, French, Swiss, Welsh, Hungarians, and Chinese. Other immigrants included Canadians, Scots, and English, who worked as masons, carpenters, roofers, and white-collar workers. By 1870, nearly one-fifth of the city's population was foreign-born.

The native-born were not all white New Englanders. Blacks arrived in Jackson almost with the earliest settlers. Thomas Trist, a blacksmith, was recorded as the first black man in the community, arriving in 1835 and building a shop somewhere west of Jackson Street. By 1870 there were 359 blacks in Jackson, many concentrated on Milwaukee Street between Michigan Avenue and Quarry Street, and southeast of Michigan Avenue and Francis Street.

The city's growth between 1870 and 1910 and its ethnic diversity can be overemphasized. Old-stock white native men still controlled commerce and politics in the town. Also, despite increased immigration, the percentage of foreign-born and blacks actually dropped during the period. While the city grew rapidly, it didn't keep pace with other Michigan cities, falling from third to seventh in the state.

Forty years after its first settlers arrived, Jackson was already showing its age. Decaying wooden buildings, interspersed with a few new three- and four-story brick buildings, lined the town's cobblestone main street from the public square to the railroad tracks. Commercial buildings, manufacturing shops, and mills were concentrated on Pearl Street (then called Luther Street), along the Grand River and near rail lines. Homes were brick or white wood-frames. The days of the log taverns had long passed.

Grain fields, orchards, and barns were still common within the city limits.

Public buildings in Jackson by 1894 included the courthouse and jail, city offices on the northeast corner of Mechanic and Cortland streets, a city hospital at the southeast corner of Ganson and Seymour streets, two fire stations, the prison, and a post office. An 1899 pamphlet noted that there was no shortage of professional legal or medical help: "... there is no occasion apparent for delays of justice, except in the facts that sixty lawyers are named in the list of the bar of the county, and that there are sixty-eight physicians in the city willing to do their best to keep litigants in fighting condition."

Jackson won a permanent home for its library in 1906, due to the philanthropy of Andrew Carnegie, the steel magnate who helped build many of the country's libraries. Zelie Emerson, a Jackson woman, persuaded Carnegie to add $20,000 to his original contribution of $50,000, and a new library was built on Michigan Avenue. Zelie Emerson's daughter, also named Zelie Emerson, and also strong-minded, was active in the suffragette movement in Great Britain, working with Sylvia Pankhurst in the fight for the right to vote.

It was during this period that the Grand River became as much a social barrier as a geographic barrier. Most of the city's wealthy became established west of the river where, particularly along Wildwood Avenue and Michigan Avenue, the city's most elegant homes were built. Most of the German, Polish, Irish, and black neighborhoods were established east of the river, where there were more modest homes and boarding houses.

By 1910, Jackson was enjoying the benefits of new technologies such as the automobile. With the benefits came problems. Stewart H. Watson had the distinction of becoming the first person in Jackson to receive a speeding ticket. On March 21, 1902, he was caught driving his Locomobile Steamer faster than six miles per hour on Michigan Avenue between East Avenue and First Street. He paid a $15 fine. Others did not heed the lesson and in 1908 Police Chief Henry L. Hunt announced a crackdown. He reported, "certain it is that automobiles are being run right along at a clip that exceeds eight miles an hour and lives and limbs are menaced."

There were also 15 miles of streetcar tracks in the city by then, as well as more than six miles of paved streets. Outside the city, roads were being improved. Spurred by bicycle enthusiasts as well as automobile buyers, the state created a highway department in 1905. Jackson County established its

Facing page, top: *Even into the 1880s and 1890s, tiny wooden storefronts dotted Jackson's main street. A shoemaker and a shoeless boy were juxtaposed in this photograph of the East End Shoe Store, 703 E. Main Street, taken about 1890. Benjamin Coldwell and John A. Sherick were the store's proprietors. Courtesy, Jackson Citizen Patriot*

Facing page, bottom: *German and Polish immigrants helped stimulate local saloon business. Stephen Kenk and his family ran this saloon adjacent to their home at 152 W. Pearl Street. It also served as a bottling works. Saloons had strong opposition from temperance people. The majority of Jackson County voters, in fact, approved a state temperance proposition in 1887. The measure was defeated statewide. Courtesy, Jackson District Library*

own road commission in 1912.

A growing city meant other problems, such as supplying water to residents and disposing of sewage. Jackson had a water works by 1874 and 30 miles of water mains with 250 hydrants by 1889. They were supplemented by the drilling of a new well field off Mansion Street in 1917. The problem of sewage disposal was attacked less successfully. The Grand River had long been a dumping place; with more people and more industry it was becoming an intolerable annoyance as well as a health hazard. What was probably the first sewage treatment plant in the city opened in 1906. For the most part it was not successful and sewage continued to be dumped into the river unchecked until 1936. By that time the state had grown weary of Jackson's inability to take care of the problem that had become a problem for every city downstream. In 1930, the city was ordered to treat its waste, and with the help of a Public Works Administration grant, a workable sewage treatment system was established at Northlawn Park in Blackman Township. The system was enlarged in 1940 and improved again in the late 1970s.

The years following 1910 brought major changes to city government. In 1914, Jackson became one of the first two dozen cities in the country to adopt the city manager form of government. The change was in name more than function, and was the outcome of a political skirmish instead of a drive for more efficient government. Under the previous aldermanic system, city government grew to be dominated by saloonkeepers and Democratic, often Catholic, eastsiders. Wealthy westside Republicans felt that too much city money was being used by the eastside aldermen solely for the purpose of strengthening their political hold on those neighborhoods. They saw the city manager form of government as a way to break the eastside domination of city government. Under the new city government, pushed by the Chamber of Commerce and local industrialists, the new five-member council would be elected at-large instead of by ward. A city manager would also be installed, but given almost no authority.

William Sparks was the first mayor under the new system and his administration's first act was to replace many Catholic city employees with Protestants, and to take away some saloon licenses. Clearly he used the new government to restore westside Republican Protestant control of city affairs.

Sparks tried in some measure to follow the theory of city manager government, but subsequent administrations reduced

Facing page, top left: *John E. Woodruff operated this horseshoeing shop in the 1890s at 408 N. Jackson Street, appropriately where latter-day automobile repair shops would spring up. Changing occupations was common in those days. Just a few years before this picture was taken Woodruff made his living as a salesman or "street broker." Courtesy, Jackson District Library*

Facing page, top right: *There seems to have been something for everyone at Duffany Brothers Bazaar. The 1887 city directory listed William M. and James H. Duffany as "dealers in music and musical merchandise, staple and fancy goods, watches, jewelry, stationery, newspapers and periodicals, also fine confectionery, fruit, etc., cigars and tobacco." Courtesy, Jackson Citizen Patriot*

Facing page, bottom: *Foote & Jenks, Inc. was a small Jackson company which began as a drug store. Foote and Jenks augmented their business by packaging flavor extracts and perfumes, eventually concentrating on flavors for beverages, ice cream, candy, and baked goods. The store is shown here on W. Michigan Avenue in 1884. Courtesy, Jackson District Library*

the city manager to little more than a messenger boy. By the early 1930s the city manager was an $1,800-a-year employee whose job was principally to wait upon councilmen, and to chauffeur for them. Under the reforms of Mayor Russell Bengel in 1935 a semblance of city manager government was restored.

The concern of westside Republicans paralleled the continued concentration of foreign-born on the east side of the city. By 1921, Page Avenue was lined with stores operated by Poles. There were also two Polish social halls. The percentage of foreign-born in the population dropped, however, during the period to 9.2 percent of a total city population of 55,187.

Meanwhile the number of blacks in the city over the period more than quadrupled, from 354 in 1910 to 1,692 in 1930. Like many northern cities, Jackson received thousands of blacks from Mississippi, Arkansas, Tennessee, Kentucky, and other southern states as demand for labor in the North increased and the supply of foreign labor diminished. The black community continued to grow in Jackson, from 3 percent of the city in 1940, to 9 percent in 1960, to 17 percent in 1980.

Signs of segregation became more apparent during the 1930s. Blacks were not always welcome in Jackson. Back in 1870, Jackson County citizens voted against a state measure giving blacks the right to vote. The measure was approved statewide. But until the 1920s there were few outward signs of segregation; neighborhoods were not as rigidly divided by race as later. By 1930 blacks were concentrated in areas between Francis Street and Page Avenue, particularly between Perrine and Summit streets south of Michigan Avenue, and blacks were excluded from the city's northeast neighborhoods.

Increased minority concentrations produced increased racial tensions in the 1960s and early 1970s. In 1963, fights broke out between white and black students at Parkside High School. Nine blacks and one white were arrested in a skirmish with police near the school. Tensions reached a high point in 1969 with the murder of Charles Cade, publisher of the *Jackson Blazer,* a newspaper that served the black community. Police concluded that the murder was committed by an associate of Cade's who later committed suicide in a Flint jail. Cade's murder occurred just a few months after a white youth was killed by a sniper, and some continued to suspect that the killing of Cade was an act of a white vigilante group.

Tensions gradually subsided after the introduction of busing to desegregate schools in 1970 and the approval the same year by the City Commission of an 11-point plan aimed at improving

Facing page, top: *John C. Bader's merchandise overflowed onto Jackson's wooden sidewalks. From this picture, taken about 1895, it seemed Bader sold everything from wringer washers to bells to oars at his store at 214 E. Main Street. Courtesy, Jackson District Library*

Facing page, bottom: *Robert Lee Green, left, a black Jackson businessman, operated a barber shop on the east side of Jackson Street, just north of Michigan Avenue, from 1904 to about 1922. In those years it was against the law to serve both white and black customers in the same shop. Green served only white customers because it was more profitable. He cut hair for black friends after hours with the shades drawn. Courtesy, Frances Williams*

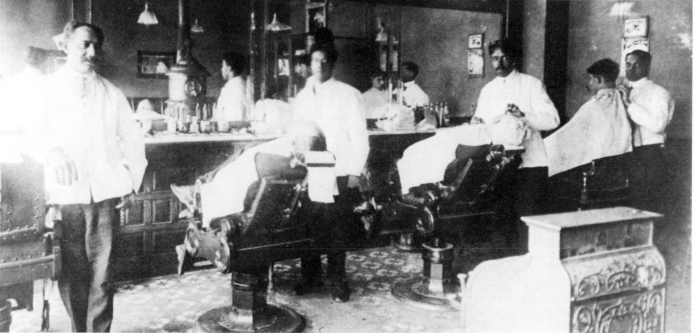

relations between blacks and whites. In 1981, the local chapter of the National Association for the Advancement of Colored People led a successful campaign to do away with the system of electing city commissioners by city-wide vote. The return to ward elections, the group felt, allowed blacks to be more fairly represented in city government.

Jackson of the 1930s began to look like a modern city. Brick, marble, and limestone skyscrapers began to dominate the downtown landscape. The city had 66 miles of paved streets by 1930. A concrete conduit was installed in the river in the mid-1930s as part of a Depression-era works project to ease Grand River pollution. The tube put the ugly, weed-choked river out of sight as it flowed through the downtown area.

As early as 1918, Jackson had an airfield at Ella Sharp Park. With the donation of land from Wiley E. Reynolds, Jackson financier, Jackson had its own modern airport west of the city in 1928. Automobile traffic congestion was more and more of a problem. In the first nine months of 1930, there were more than 11 deaths and 254 traffic injuries in the city.

After 1930, Jackson saw increased suburbanization as the development of the townships increased. From 1930 to 1980 the city population dropped from 55,187 to 39,739, while the county as a whole grew from 92,304 to 151,925. Between 1970 and 1980 alone some townships such as Rives, Grass Lake, and Columbus enjoyed population increases of more than 40 percent.

Suburbanization brought the development of shopping centers out of the downtown area. Paka Plaza, in the city's northwest quadrant, opened in 1965. Westwood Mall was completed in 1972 at the northwest corner of Michigan Avenue and Brown Street.

Meanwhile, the downtown underwent wrenching changes. Beginning in 1960, urban renewal reshaped two major areas of the city. The first urban renewal project in Jackson was the Belden Urban Renewal Project, a 157-acre area southeast of the central business district between Franklin and High streets, east of Francis Street. The government acquired and demolished 379 buildings, renovated another 200, relocated 200 families, and sold 8.5 acres for apartment housing.

The second project involved what was called the East Michigan Central Business District. This included 20 acres in a downtown area between Francis Street and the railroad tracks to the east. As urban renewal was going on, the city also changed its downtown traffic pattern and built a downtown pedestrian mall called Progress Place Mall. In a move that planners hoped

Four people were murdered November 21, 1883, at the farmhouse of Jacob Crouch, making front page headlines as far away as Detroit and Chicago, and launching years of investigations. Henry White, above, Crouch's son-in-law, was killed along with his wife Eunice, her father Jacob, and Moses Polley, a cattle buyer visiting from Pennsylvania. Only a farmhand and a servant were spared. Courtesy, Dr. Byrne M. Daly

Jacob Crouch, a wealthy Spring Arbor farmer, was as wary of cameras as he was of banks, and did not allow pictures to be taken of him. This picture was taken after his death, and the eyeballs were penciled in. Crouch was widely known to have kept his cash in his house, but neither Crouch's fortune, nor Moses Polley's sizeable bankroll, were stolen the night of the murders. Courtesy, Dr. Byrne M. Daly

Eunice Crouch White was eight months pregnant at the time of the notorious Crouch murders. The youngest daughter of Jacob Crouch, she was believed to be his favorite and destined to inherit his fortune. Some speculated the murders were done by jealous family members, and the most prominent suspect was her brother Judd. The murders were never solved, and Judd maintained his innocence for the rest of his life. Courtesy, Dr. Byrne M. Daly

would relieve traffic congestion and help downtown business, Michigan Avenue from Mechanic Street to Blackstone Street was blocked off and a landscaped pedestrian area created. Traffic was rerouted on widened one-way streets north and south of the central business district. A Chamber of Commerce publication boasted about the changes:

It's difficult to estimate the importance of Progress Place Mall to the economy of Jackson, but it's not hard to determine the attitude of people who shop downtown; they love it. The beautifully landscaped mall and its companion piece, the $6 million Central Business District Perimeter Traffic Loop, have provided an infusion of beauty, vitality, and convenience that has boosted the morale of the city, reduced the blood pressure of the shoppers and increased profits of retailers.

Not everybody loved it, however. The mall was controversial from the start and many blamed it for further deterioration of the downtown. They argued that it forced traffic away from downtown and made downtown driving more confusing. By 1969, vacant stores lined downtown commercial streets. The mall was removed bit by bit and by 1983 two-way traffic was fully restored on the main downtown street. The changes brought by urban renewal and subsequent downtown building left Michigan Avenue west of the river cut off forever from Michigan Avenue east of the river.

The downtown seemed a symbol for the whole community as it entered the 1980s: mature, with a rich history, but showing its age and its infirmities. The community seemed to be groping for new directions. Some looked to the past and wondered if the future would hold the same wealth of opportunities. The town had seen so many changes, changes at a speed and scope unimaginable to the pioneers who fired guns in celebration or wept in despair upon finding themselves in the new settlement. New industry, new technology, new people, and new ways of living continually reshaped the character of the place. If the past gave up any lessons for the future, those lessons would be that continued change, sometimes reassuring, sometimes frightening, would give Jackson many more opportunities to build a better place to work and live. It is both exciting and disconcerting to realize that Jackson will see as much change in its second 150 years as in its first.

Facing page, top left: *Horse-drawn sleighs kept commerce moving in winter in the 19th and early 20th centuries. This one pictured along Page Avenue around 1920 may have been carrying barrels of sauerkraut. Courtesy, Frank Machnik Collection*

Facing page, top right: *Maher Brothers Music Store was one of downtown Jackson's shops near the turn of the century. The store survived into the late 1920s, offering Victrolas and radios in addition to pianos and organs. (MHC, BHL, UM)*

Facing page, bottom: *The 1914 city directory listed Albert E. Nicholls' meat market at 225 W. Main Street. An ice box is at the rear of the store. For sanitary reasons, butchers were not allowed to handle money. Customers paid at the booth to the left. (MHC, BHL, UM)*

Above: *The Merriman house, built about 1860, is an early example of the fine homes built on the west side of the city. Mary W. Merriman, mother of Ella Sharp, lived in the house for about 10 years in the late 19th century. Among its owners were Michael Shoemaker, a prominent Jackson citizen and state legislator. The Italianate house survived into the 1980s. (MHC, BHL, UM)*

Right: *E.A. Webster, president of the Austin, Tomlinson and Webster Manufacturing Company, was a great promoter of the company's Jackson wagons, particularly at state and county fairs. No doubt this group's repertoire included the "Old Jackson Wagon Song" and its refrain: "Buy one, I say, buy one, buy a Jackson today, today." (MHC, BHL, UM)*

Below: *Clark's Lake has been a favorite getaway spot in Jackson for a long time, as this turn-of-the-century view of Clark Lake Yacht Club indicates. Courtesy, Thomas A. Johnson*

Below, right: *This Jackson County barn bears an advertising message from long ago. Courtesy, Mary E. Abbott*

Clockwise from top left: *Distinctive archi-tecture lends a picturesque quality to Jackson. This well-maintained barn presents a red-and-white contrast in the snow; the bell tower of St. Mary's Church is a dramatic* landmark; *the cupola of the Ella Sharp Museum is a graceful memory of an era gone by, as is this ornate cupola from a Victorian mansion on First Street. Courtesy, Mary E. Abbott*

Facing page, right: *The settlers' log cabin at Ella Sharp Park has been painstakingly restored inside and out to provide an accurate picture of pioneer life in Jackson.* Facing page, left: *The lane leading to Ella Sharp's farm seems to lead to the 19th century. Courtesy, Mary E. Abbott*

Top, left: *Loredo Taft's lovely "Memory" looks out onto the autumn landscape of Woodland. Courtesy, Mary E. Abbott*

Top, right: *This old barn rests on a hand-built stone foundation. Courtesy, Mary E. Abbott*

Bottom: *Sparks Foundation County Park offers a shady vista on a summer day. Courtesy, Gladys L. Porter*

Left: *The woods near the Ella Sharp Museum become vivid in the fall.* Below: *Cascades Park is a fragile sculpture of hoarfrost on New Year's Day in 1980. Courtesy, Mary E. Abbott*

Visitors are silhouetted by the Cascades, a man-made illuminated waterfall built by William Sparks. The Cascades are among the most popular attractions in Jackson. Courtesy, Gladys L. Porter

Clockwise from top left: *Boys experiment*
with computers at the Jackson District
Library. Courtesy, Mary E. Abbott
The Harvest Festival at the Ella Sharp
Museum gives this young boy a close-up look
at a pumpkin almost bigger than he is.
Courtesy, Mary E. Abbott

"Summer Night Tree" by Louise Nevelson
becomes a playground for these young
art-lovers. Courtesy, Mary E. Abbott
Jackson turns out to applaud the Jackson
High School marching band on parade.
Courtesy, Gladys L. Porter

Consider the 1917 HOLLIER
Before you contract for 1917

CHAPTER SIX

Partners in Progress

By Patricia McEnroe Koschik

Facing page: The Hollier was briefly manufactured in Jackson. Courtesy, Lloyd Ganton

Over its span of more than 150 years, Jackson, Michigan, has had its ups and downs, experiencing both periods of great prosperity and times of economic hardship. More than once in its past, Jackson has suffered economic depression and survived.

When the railroad car repair shops with their thousands of jobs were closed, the community was shaken but rebounded. The demise of the fashion corset manufacturing industry, of which Jackson was once a leader, was overcome. And the Great Depression, when nearly one-third of the city's families were on relief, only led to the strong financial gains of the 1940s and the economic stability that lasted through the 1970s.

Jackson has survived because of what it has to offer its people. Though the early 1980s were troubled by business closings, high unemployment, and decreasing revenues, Jackson's future must be viewed in terms of historical perspective and the qualities that will enable it to prosper in better times to come.

The city's location in the state allows it to conveniently supply goods and services to most large cities in Michigan, and its excellent highway and rail connections make it convenient to major markets in the United States and Canada. Its work force, divergent in ethnic backgrounds and talents, provides industrious, skilled, and loyal labor to staff its wide variety of enterprises.

Manufacturing has been the chief occupation of the city since its establishment. By 1836 a company engaged in plows and castings was begun; and in 1842 a wagon manufacturer opened his shop. Jackson's products are wide in range. While many are related to the automobile industry nearby, others vary from basic machine parts to space age robotics.

The city is more than a manufacturing hub. Service companies provide, for example, sophisticated engineering skills, financial expertise, energy for much of the state, and new options in housing. Its school system is topped with a community college, four-year private college, and a private business institute to offer higher learning. Two hospitals — one brand new and the other newly remodeled — make health care in Jackson as advanced as in any city its size.

Jackson offers much in its quality of life. Tourism is

becoming a bigger endeavor as the region increases the marketing of its attractions. Not only does the community have an abundance of lakes, park land, golf courses, a harness raceway, and a major professional auto raceway, it also offers more in the arts than most comparable cities. Its museum, symphony, and theatrical groups are a source of pride.

The following section details some of the industries, businesses, and institutions that make up Jackson's heritage and strength. Their histories are worth telling, for they provide the foundation for Jackson's future, and demonstrate that even in hardship there is progress.

This man and his pushcart was a pleasant summer sight for ice cream lovers on Jackson's east side in the 1920s. Starting in 1942, Jackson became a haven for ice cream fanciers. That was the year Loud & Jackson Dairy added ice cream operations to its plant. Loud & Jackson eventually became Jackson All Star Dairy and the ice cream counter became simply The Parlour, a very popular ice cream shop. Courtesy, Frank Machnik Collection

GREATER JACKSON CHAMBER OF COMMERCE

Since its origin in 1909 the Greater Jackson Chamber of Commerce has actively led a number of campaigns, and has served as a catalyst to assist in making Jackson a better place in which to live and work. For example, the very form of city government, the commission-manager system, was adopted because business leaders demanded reform and the Chamber spearheaded the change.

The Chamber enables its 400-plus members, both business and professional, to accomplish collectively what no one could do individually. Recent growth in membership has been noteworthy as the organization has broadened its focus to encompass four main areas of effort.

The Chamber provides economic and demographic information to prospective business firms. In the mid-1980s a Center for Defense Procurements was established to help local businesses obtain government contracts. The Senior Corps of Retired Executives (SCORE) in its first year matched 10 retired but skilled former managers with more than 50 local clients to share the retirees' expertise. The organization is also involved in Jackson's Alliance for Business Development, an umbrella organization of area groups seeking to attract and retain businesses. An innovative Business Incubator Program provides "birthing" and nurturing for newly developing firms.

The Chamber also works to see that the interests of business are represented when local and state officials are elected. It supports some candidates financially through its political action committee, as well.

To provide economic understanding, education, and training, the Chamber works with the public schools and the community college to introduce students to the free-enterprise

system and their future roles in it.

Tourism and conventions have always been a focus for the Chamber. Thousands of inquiries for travel information are answered each year, and the organization's efforts helped bring more than 30,000 visitors to the community in 1983.

Today's efforts are more sophisticated than those of the 1909 Chamber, but the organization has always promoted the best interests of the city and county. In addition to helping change the system of government in 1914, the Chamber had the name of Main Street changed to Michigan Avenue. It also helped achieve improved telephone and telegraph service.

For a few years during the financially disastrous early 1930s, the Chamber of Commerce was inactive. Later, beginning with only $1.51 in its treasury, it went on to secure new industries for Jackson, helped launch the first Community Chest campaign, worked to place Foote Hospital under control of a civilian

board, and heavily promoted tourism.

In the 1950s the group helped form the Jackson Area Industrial Development Corporation, and a decade later helped campaign to have a city income tax approved by voters. Other examples of Chamber involvement include the formation of the Downtown Development Authority and the Jackson County Rose Festival.

As the Chamber looks ahead, it plans additional programs of business assistance. It also intends to seek nationwide attention for Jackson's attractions in the entertainment field by boosting the city's theater, space center, and other entertainment facilities. If its efforts prove fruitful, the Greater Jackson Chamber of Commerce will succeed in promoting the city as the entertainment center of the Midwest.

The Greater Jackson Chamber of Commerce has been serving the citizens of the community since 1909. Today it is situated at 401 South Jackson Street.

JACKSON BUSINESS INSTITUTE

Jackson's famous Zouaves drill team, shown here at Niagara Falls in 1905, had its beginning in 1890 at the business school. Officers in center are Captain William Sparks and Lieutenant William Corbett, longtime team leaders. Photo courtesy of the Jackson Citizen Patriot.

The voices of America's theatrical giants are no longer heard in the former Athenaeum Theater, once a stop on the legitimate theater circuit. Now the stone building at the corner of Mechanic and Washington resounds with young voices, the muted taps of electric typewriters, and the rustle of stenographers' notebooks.

Jackson Business Institute, which began life in 1867 as a "mercantile education institution," found a permanent home in the large stone structure in 1928, after being housed in several other Jackson locations. Among its many uses, the building, named the Bloomfield Block, held the city library and served as the entrance and lobby of the old Athenaeum Theater next door. Famous for its performances by such greats as Sarah Bernhardt and Ethel Barrymore, the Athenaeum later featured travelogs and silent movies. The facility was later sold and renamed the Majestic, and finally the theater part of the building was demolished.

General George M. Devlin founded Jackson Business Institute's forerunner, the Devlin Business College, when he was a young man in his early twenties, just home from the Civil War. He is also remembered as the founder of the colorful Jackson Zouaves, organized in 1890 among cadets at the business college. They established an international reputation as a crack drill and marching team, a reputation that continued even after it was no longer associated with the school. Led for many years by Captain William Sparks, the Zouaves became the drill team for the Jackson Elks Lodge and later as a consolidated team that represented the American Legion.

The first courses offered by Devlin's school were bookkeeping, penmanship, commercial law, arithmetic, banking, commission, forwarding, and business correspondence. So great was the demand for telegraphers that in 1871 the college opened a telegraphy department for the training of the communications specialties. "There is no fear of overstocking the market for telegraph operators," the college promised.

As that early school met the demands of the business world in 1871, so has Jackson Business Institute tried to meet changing business needs over the years. Up-to-date word-processing training is now part of the current curriculum, which includes courses in auditing, management, cost accounting, labor relations, and communications, as well as the traditional shorthand and typing.

Day and evening classes are offered to about 300 students a year, many of whom are working toward a 12-month certificate or an 18- or 24-month diploma in 10 different programs that prepare them for jobs or transfer to four-year colleges. The school is accredited by the Association of Independent Colleges and Schools.

Jackson Business Institute has a history of well-qualified administrators and faculty members. Owners of the school, notably J.A. Ebersol and A.C. Hermann, brought with them experience from other commercial schools and from the business world.

Jackson native Jack D. Bunce, the current president, came to that position after 13 years' experience in business. He authored the school's name change in 1983, from Jackson Business University to Jackson Business Institute, while also arranging its structure to nonprofit status. Bunce and his wife, Sally, returned to Jackson from California in 1974 to take over management of the college.

The Bloomfield Block, built to house the public library and lobby of the Athenaeum Theater, is now the home of Jackson Business Institute. Photo from the Ella Sharp Museum files.

HARRIS-McBURNEY COMPANY

Before the Harris-McBurney Company developed a specialty in telecommunications, it handled a full range of utility line functions such as installing and maintaining traffic signals in downtown Jackson.

Harris-McBurney Company works all over the United States but keeps its corporate headquarters in Jackson because it's "home."

As a public utility contractor, Harris-McBurney has grown from a small venture installing power lines for rural electrification to a nation-wide contracting firm that installs sophisticated telecommunications systems and handles peak service work for telephone companies.

Frederic R. Harris and Arthur J. McBurney founded their new organization in 1935 with a work force of 12 employees and a weekly payroll of about $250. McBurney supplied the financing while Harris supplied the know-how. An electrical engineer, Harris had been the first chief engineer of the Michigan Public Utilities Commission before coming to Jackson as city manager.

When the Depression hit, Harris was president of the Jackson Construction Co., which had been very successful, but was devastated by the hard times. When the opportunity to work on the federal project providing electrical wiring to

rural areas came along, Harris established the new firm.

Harris' son, Charles "Bucky" Harris, began part-time work for his father at the age of 14 for 25 cents per hour, serving as a lineman in the summer. During World War II the younger Harris served in the Signal Corps, where he acquired skills in telecommunications. After the war he joined the company, purchasing McBurney's ownership in the firm. In 1957 he bought his father's share of the business and is now its president and sole owner. Frederic R. Harris died 1962 at the age of 72.

Bucky Harris' experience in telecommunications affected the later direction of his company. Though its early years brought much work in airport runway lighting and installation of electrical cables, the firm had developed a specialty in telecommunications work by the substantial growth years of the 1950s.

Harris-McBurney has worked for all major telephone companies in the United States, serving as an extension of the work force during boom times when the telephone companies have more work than they can handle.

Most of Harris-McBurney's work in recent years has been in the South and in the West, where new construction has demanded extra help in installing and splicing cables,

setting up general office switches, and maintaining telephone equipment. Regional offices of the firm are located in Tampa, Florida; Pomona, California; Virginia Beach, Virginia; and Bryan, Texas.

While Harris-McBurney works for telephone companies on a yearly basis with permanent crews, Harris-McBurney Services, Inc., is the subsidiary that handles one-time projects involving large telecommunications system. The subsidiary, with one regional office in Castro Valley, California, has installed systems for the Miami International Airport and Jackson's new W.A. Foote Memorial Hospital, among others.

Both the firm and its subsidiary are service organizations, working with the manufacturers of equipment or the telephone companies that hire them. Though about 600 people are employed full time, another 2,000 may be hired on a temporary basis over the course of a year.

The Harris-McBurney Company occupies three floors of the Harris Building, a 14-story office facility constructed in 1926 for Wiley R. Reynolds, a Jackson industrialist. It is located at 180 West Michigan Avenue.

One man using up-to-date equipment can lay telephone cable now, a job that once required four workers.

DAWN FOOD PRODUCTS, INC.

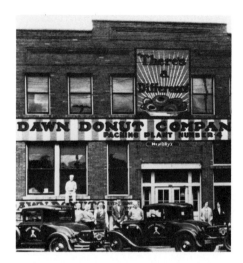

Dawn's staff, in front of the plant when it was located at 330 Otsego, helped develop the first patented baking mix process. Photo circa 1930.

Not surprisingly for a Jackson-owned and -operated business, there's a family atmosphere at Dawn Food Products, Inc. "Everybody has a feeling of involvement in the company. The whole operation is the Dawn family," says Ronald L. Jones, president of the firm which manufactures a variety of baking mixes and baking equipment.

Jones and his brothers, Steven M., executive vice-president, and Miles E., vice-president of operations, grew up with the business. During summer vacations they unloaded boxcars of sugar and worked in the plant making baking mixes. The family recently showed its commitment to Jackson by hiring only Jackson-area firms to design and build a million-dollar expansion to Dawn's facilities at 2021 Micor Drive.

This strong family feeling was the organization's cornerstone laid by the Joneses' father, the late E. Marlin Jones, who purchased control of Dawn in 1955. At that time, Dawn—named for the time of day when doughnuts are made—already was an established firm with a good

reputation. Eugene Worden and Grover Lutz of Union City had opened the Century Bakery at 112 East Michigan, a location that was large enough for the bakery but not large enough for the manufacturing of mixes that were beginning to be sold.

As word of the establishment's doughnuts spread, bakers in neighboring communities began pressing for the mixes. Demand for the Dawn mixes became so large that the bakery was closed and the nation's first industrial mix company was formed at 326-330 Otsego in 1920.

Marlin Jones joined Dawn in 1936 and helped the firm through the war years when commodities were scarce. Traveling to agricultural areas, he arranged with farmers to commit their fields of grain to Dawn for food production.

The city's plans for a downtown perimeter route, whose planned path traveled right through Dawn's location, prompted the company to build a new plant in Jackson's Micor Industrial Park. The new building, occupied early in 1967, featured three floors of production and office area with a mixing tower five floors high.

Dawn Food Products has expanded far beyond its original doughnut mix operation. Today it supplies 150 different bakery mix products to customers in the United States and abroad. Dawn Equipment Co., begun in 1957, accounts for all of the bakery equipment sales for Dawn Manufacturing bakery fryers that produce 400 doughnuts a minute as well as automatic icing and glazing machines are its specialty. Complete bakery installation can be furnished by this division.

Under Marlin Jones' direction, Dawn's annual sales increased from less than one million dollars to

some $27 million. "The employees are responsible for the success of the firm," states Jones. And this concept combines with added sales each year. Dawn is in the top five among the country's industrial bakery mix suppliers.

In one week's time, Dawn receives and uses more than one million pounds of flours, 300,000 pounds of sugars, 20 different kinds of shortening products, and spices from as far away as East India. Quality-control measures follow the production process. Since the key to Dawn's success has been mixes that work the same way every time, a sample of the baking mix is pulled from each batch for testing. However, it's only in the product laboratory that Dawn turns out finished doughnuts. The retail Dawn Donut Shops are owned by a franchiser that operates them under a licensing arrangement for the Dawn name. The company's influence extends worldwide, as well, by holding licensing agreements with firms in Japan and Canada to produce mixes from its formulas.

In recent years Dawn Food Products has added a new warehouse to its plant in Micor Industrial Park as well as a million-dollar addition to give the firm more office and research and development space.

COMERICA BANK-JACKSON

Appropriately for a financial institution, Comerica Bank-Jackson is the sum of many parts. It is the product of mergers and consolidations of a number of Jackson-area banking establishments with roots going back to just after the Civil War.

The institution's most recent merger took place in 1982 when its forerunner, The National Bank of Jackson, joined with Detroitbank Corporation, a bank holding company. The parent company and all its subsidiaries took on the common corporate name of Comerica that same year.

Today Comerica Bank-Jackson has deposits of more than $263 million, with almost 400 employees in 18 offices throughout, and even beyond, Jackson County. The merger made it part of one of the 40 largest banks in the country. Comerica subsidiaries throughout the state of Michigan, and in Florida, Ohio, Canada, and England provide customers with the most comprehensive financial services available.

The size and services of Comerica Bank are a far cry from those of the original The National Bank of Jackson when it opened its doors in August 1933, with deposits of $505,523 and 22 employees. The National Bank had been formed from the ashes of prior Jackson banking institutions.

The origins date from 1865, when the Peoples National Bank was chartered by a group of Jackson business leaders headed by longtime merchant Wiley R. Reynolds. Another predecessor, the Union Bank, had opened in 1884 with capital of $100,000 and General W.L. Withington as its first president. Through a 1927 merger, it was renamed the National Union Bank and Trust Company.

Leaders of the two institutions, the Peoples National Bank and the National Union Bank, agreed to merge. They formed the Union and Peoples National Bank and moved into a new, million-dollar, 17-story building at 120 West Michigan Avenue on March 29, 1930.

Though the building was hailed as a "shaft of strength," the bank weakened, suffering the effects of the worsening Depression. Governor W.A. Comstock declared a statewide bank holiday in February 1933, and a month later the institution was placed under the control of a conservator, Stuart M. Schram.

The National Bank of Jackson was organized as the successor to the Union and Peoples National Bank. With a $200,000 loan from the federal Reconstruction Finance Corporation and another $200,000 raised locally as capital, a partial release of frozen deposits was made possible. Schram, a prominent motor car agency owner, was named the institution's first president.

Operations continued in the original building, though The National Bank never took ownership. Now called the Jackson County Tower Building, the structure was placed in receivership, along with other assets, and was sold in 1937 for $160,000.

The National Bank became one of the leading financial institutions in the area. In 1960 its new headquarters was completed, a $1.5-million, four-story bank building at 245 West Michigan. Bank employees, 75 moving men, and 42 heavily armed police officers transferred $100 million in cash, securities, and other assets over a weekend.

Over the years the bank consolidated with smaller institutions, opened branch offices, introduced the first automatic teller machines in Jackson, and was one of the pioneers in electronic banking.

As Comerica Bank-Jackson, headed by president Robert W. Ballantine and chairman of the board Robert L. Condon, the financial institution faces a period of great change in the financial world. Increased competition, deregulation, higher technologies, and changing customer requirements are necessitating new strategies and structures of an industry whose future promises to differ greatly from its past.

Now called the Jackson County Tower Building, this 17-story building was the original home of Comerica's predecessor, The National Bank of Jackson.

INN ON JACKSON SQUARE

Downtown Jackson has always had at least one prominent hotel—the Hibbard House, the Dalton, the Otsego, and the Hayes all had stature in their day. The Inn on Jackson Square is the latest in that proud line. After a muddled start under frequently changing leadership, new owners and new management are striving to build the community respect that a quality downtown hotel must have.

As coincidence would have it, the Inn on Jackson Square stands on the approximate site of a former hotel. In the early 1900s the Dal-Van Hotel was advertised as an "absolutely fireproof," seven-story hotel at 132 East Michigan. The structure existed for many years there, changing its name a few times along the way, until much of that portion of eastern downtown Jackson was deemed blighted and fell to the urban renewal wrecker's ball.

While a number of projects were proposed and rejected for the site, the land stood vacant for about 10 years. In 1974 Jackson Square Associates was formed by Mario and Vallentino Collavino of Windsor, Ontario, and a $10-million development was begun. Included in the plans were an 11-story office building to be occupied principally by City Bank and Trust Company, a 160-room, 10-story Sheraton hotel, a one-story mall of shops and offices connecting the two buildings, and an underground garage for parking.

The hotel's grand opening was in January 1977, and 14 conventions were booked in advance for the first year. The Collavinos hired a management firm from New York to run the Sheraton franchise operation, but the manager sent to Jackson to staff and stock the new hotel was transferred even before the opening, a pattern that was to continue. Frequent changes in management firms and managers resulted in an opening operation that lost money at the rate of $30,000 to $40,000 a month.

This was the hotel's situation when the Jackson Square complex was sold for $8.4 million in 1983 to a group of private investors headed by Southfield attorney Stuart M. Kaufman. No longer a Sheraton, it has been renamed Inn on Jackson Square, and management was taken over by Consolidated Hotel Management of Toronto, a firm that oversees operations at a number of independent hotels. Irving S. Phillips, an experienced hotel troubleshooter, was sent in to take the mismanaged enterprise and put it on a profitable footing.

Consolidated Hotel Management immediately instituted needed inventory controls, inspections, and training of staff members. Changes are under way for the bedrooms, the lobby, the dining room, the convention and banquet rooms, and recreational facilities. Most important, the new management is working at regaining friends in Jackson, the local business that was lost during the hotel's first six years.

Jackson area residents know the Inn on Jackson Square has much to offer with its attractive dining room, its comfortable library lounge, and spacious meeting rooms that can accommodate small groups or as many as 650 persons. The current owners and management of the hotel are doing their best to meet the community's expectations. They are confident that, over time, the Inn on Jackson Square will live up to the reputations of its predecessors.

Summer Night Tree, *a 30-foot tall steel sculpture by artist Louise Nevelson, graces the Jackson Square plaza. The sculpture was made possible by a $52,000 grant from the National Endowment for the Arts and $102,000 in private contributions. Photo courtesy of the* Jackson Citizen Patriot.

CAMSHAFT MACHINE COMPANY

World War II was fought in part by businesses at home that turned out military tanks and trucks, ammunition, and aircraft.

Camshaft Machine Company traces its origin to that war effort. Harold F. Andrews was a stockbroker who had been a World War I Army Air Corps pilot. Herman W. Melling was an engineer and inventor. B. Frank Titus was a skilled camshaft maker for Motor Shaft—a firm that became Muskegon Motor Specialties of Jackson.

The three men, along with Otto H. Schultz who was part owner for a short time, founded Camshaft Machine Company on June 16, 1942, to make camshafts for military and other engines.

Many of the key employees came from Motor Shaft because it was rumored that concern was going to move its camshaft division out of Jackson. A lathe man, an inspector, two grinders, and a drilling and tapping specialist were among the 10 or so employees who went to work in a rented barn/chicken coop. The T-shaped building was of double-walled brick, constructed by convict labor in the 1920s.

Camshaft rented that property at 717 Woodworth Road for many years. Eventually it bought the building and land, added adjacent property, and expanded its plant size. The firm has produced mainly camshafts since its beginning, but has also manufactured other engine parts which require precision grinding. Its first customers were Ranger Aircraft, Hercules Motors, Lycoming Aircraft, and Caterpillar Tractor.

Both steel and cast-iron camshafts are made, and production is about evenly divided between original equipment used by companies such as Caterpillar, Ford, General Motors, Chrysler, and Allis-Chalmers, and

replacement parts used by firms such as Dana Corporation, TRW, Sealed Power, Melling Tool, and Wolverine Gear.

Camshaft Machine is a privately held concern owned by the families of the three founders. When its present chief executive, Harold P. (Andy) Andrews, Harold F. Andrews' son, joined the organization in 1964 after 10 years' experience in other businesses, yearly sales were about one million dollars. That figure has grown to exceed $40 million, and the firm now has subsidiaries elsewhere.

In August 1970 the main Camshaft building was gutted by a devastating fire that caused about one million dollars in damage, destroying its 35 to 40 cam-grinding machines. While the fire was still burning, company officials telephoned around the country and put a hold on every camshaft cam grinder that was for sale. They bought some and borrowed others and within a week were in

production again, working seven days a week, 24 hours a day, in the unburned warehouse and in the parking lot.

Fortunately for Camshaft, the warehouse was untouched by the fire, so its inventory of 73,000 to 75,000 finished parts ready to ship was unharmed. The firm was able to supply its customers at about 90 to 95 percent efficiency.

Camshaft Machine rebuilt its plant to the newest specifications and stocked it with the best machinery available. Since then, it has grown by a series of additions to a 128,000-square-foot plant with a capacity in excess of 100,000 camshafts a month. The firm employs more than 240 people in a stable non-union atmosphere. Producing approximately 400 different parts and serving about 100 customers, Camshaft Machine Company is the largest independent manufacturer of engine camshafts in the United States.

In 1942 Camshaft was started in a rented barn/chicken coop (inset). Following the 1970 fire that devastated Camshaft's main building, the firm rebuilt and has expanded to become the largest independent manufacturer of engine camshafts in the country.

Founders Herman W. Melling, Harold F. Andrews, and B. Frank Titus began their new firm on June 16, 1942, to manufacture camshafts for military vehicles. Photo circa 1950.

CAMP INTERNATIONAL, INC.

Though Jackson was the corset capital of the West around the turn of the century, only one of those early manufacturing firms has survived.

Camp International, Inc., has outgrown its one-room-shop beginnings and today thrives as a multimillion-dollar worldwide company selling more than 1,300 products through 5,300 outlets. It was able to survive and flourish by changing its product line. Shortly after World War II, when new fibers revolutionized women's foundation garments, Camp management decided to focus on surgical support products instead of fashion garments.

The organization now registers sales of more than $40 million a year in orthotic and prosthetic items—that is, products that support the body or that artificially replace body parts.

Samuel Higby Camp, the founder, was born in 1871 in a log cabin. As a young man, he managed two other Jackson corset businesses, including the Bortree Manufacturing Company, the first corset factory west of New York City. On January 1, 1908, he opened his own firm, S.H. Camp and Company.

Camp's first important product was called the Goodwin corset, a boned front-lace model described in sales literature as "an anatomically correct garment modeled more upon the lines of sculpture than on the usual conventional lines of corsetry." The Goodwin corset was endorsed by world-famous singing star Anna Held.

In 1919 Samuel H. Camp filed for a patent for an eyeletted buckle, his invention that allowed him to offer the "Camco corset for reducing and supporting, with back lace in 11 different types with Camp patented adjustment." His competitors criticized the buckle for the next 17

years until the patents expired— then most of them copied it.

The 1920s were a decade of innovation. Camp developed and patented the continuous-lacing principle. Together with the eyeletted buckle, the lacing allowed an even adjustment of a garment, providing precise support and fit of physiological belts, braces, and corsets.

Camp moved his factory a number of times, once to acquire larger quarters, once to improve the company's location, and later, in 1927, because of a fire that devastated the plant as well as all the garments and raw materials. The firm found temporary quarters and began delivering finished products within two weeks. A few months later the enterprise found a permanent home at 109 West Washington Street in the former American Lady Corset Company building.

Camp's first international connection came in 1929, when the company had about 200 employees and annual sales of about one million dollars. Berlei, of Australia and New Zealand, became its first overseas licensee. A subsidiary in Windsor, Ontario, was established in 1932 to serve Canada and to export to England.

During World War II Camp was

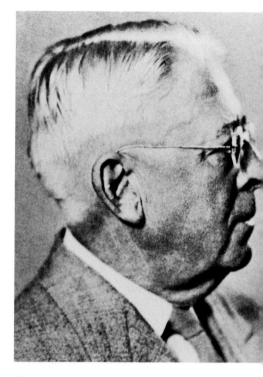

Samuel Higby Camp, founder of Camp International, Inc.

limited in its production because materials were scarce, but was more fortunate than other garment makers because of the medical nature of its products. Rationing boards gave the company priorities

S.H. Camp Company occupied part of this building in the 1920s.

when shown hundreds of prescriptions for surgical items, and Camp's business increased during the war years. Women bought Camp supports when they could not get other foundation garments, and they begged for more.

After the war, when synthetic fibers were changing the foundation industry, Camp management decided to focus on the surgical support field. The company increased its research and participation in the medical field and added a broad new range of products, including a larger line of supports for men.

In November 1944 Samuel Higby Camp, age 78, and his wife, Margaret Hammond Camp, were hit by an automobile while walking near their home at 775 West Michigan Avenue. They died 10 days later—18 minutes apart—and were memorialized through the Samuel Higby Camp Foundation, established in 1951 by Camp's sister, Donna Camp. Samuel Camp was succeeded as president by Christian H. Fleck, who served until his death in 1947, and then by Henry C. Menke, a boyhood friend and business associate.

Forrest I. Yeakey became president in 1951 and led the company through many years of international and domestic expansion. Under his leadership, a number of licensees and subsidiaries were formed in England, the Netherlands, Scandinavia, Switzerland, and Spain. Yeakey, who in 1983 marked 50 years of service to the company, became honorary chairman of the board in 1967, the year Richard B. Firestone was elected president and chairman of the board.

Camp International, the new corporate name acquired in 1973, has continued to add foreign offshoots and has expanded at home as well. In 1984 its plant, located in the Micor Industrial Park, was

enlarged to 72,000 squre feet. All manufacturing, shipping, and receiving take place at this site, while the corporate offices remain at 109 West Washington. The firm's employees number about 330 locally and more than 750 overall.

The present line of Camp products includes a full range of prostheses and garments for the post-mastectomy woman. Supports are the firm's oldest products and are available for every part of the body. Camp is the world leader in the conservative treatment of low-back pain with its back supports and its recommendations for correlated orthotic treatments. Other notable products include elastic stockings for patients with venous disorders, rigid spinal braces, and traction equipment, as well as special apparatus for those injured in sports. Among Camp's newest products are a rotating disk used for ankle rehabilitation and a shoulder

brace for post-stroke patients that permits more mobility of the affected side of the body.

The company sponsors medical research by physicians and medical schools to keep pace with advances in medical theories and treatments, and regularly brings its own technicians together from around the world to exchange information.

Camp International, Inc., the largest distributor and manufacturer of orthotic and prosthetic products in the world, has a tradition of innovations in materials, products, and marketing methods, all intended to live up to the company's motto: *Validos Unimus—Invalidis Servimus*—"We shield the strong—We serve the weak."

The continuous-lacing principle, patented by Camp, allowed proper corset fit of any form.

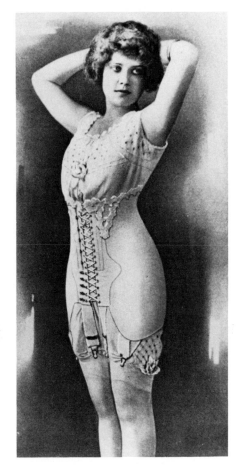

An early advertisement for Camco corsets emphasized how the body could be molded to graceful proportions "with utmost ease and simplicity."

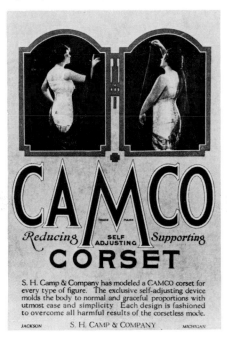

CAMCO
Reducing SELF ADJUSTING *Supporting*
CORSET

S. H. Camp & Company has modeled a CAMCO corset for every type of figure. The exclusive self-adjusting device molds the body to normal and graceful proportions with utmost ease and simplicity Each design is fashioned to overcome all harmful results of the corsetless mode.

JACKSON   S. H. CAMP & COMPANY   MICHIGAN

COMMONWEALTH ASSOCIATES INC.

William C. Fargo, one of the co-founders of what became Commonwealth Associates Inc., seated in a dinghy atop a riverboat with a group of engineers and developers, scouting sites for hydroelectric dams along the AuSable River. Photo courtesy of Consumers Power Company.

As a company magazine published in the 1970s described it, "The history of Commonwealth closely parallels that of the electric and gas industries in the United States." The roots of Commonwealth Associates Inc., located at 209 East Washington Avenue, go back to the 1880s.

The firm's reputation is built on a rich tradition of research and innovation in the generation and distribution of power. Today it is the major subsidiary of Gilbert Associates, Inc., a leading consulting engineering concern, known throughout the world and ranking among the largest in the United States.

Gilbert/Commonwealth, as the local firm identifies itself, has about 1,100 employees working out of the Jackson office. Although the company's stock is traded publicly, the major stockholders are employees who own shares in the firm. Under its charter, only the stockholders who are employees may vote to elect the company's board of directors.

Gilbert/Commonwealth's product is professional engineering, consulting, and construction management services. Its clients are electric and gas utilities, manufacturing and process industries, and government agencies throughout the world.

Among the projects in which the Gilbert firms are involved are major nuclear- and fossil-fueled electric generating plants, electric transmission and distribution systems, and, increasingly, the advancement of tomorrow's most promising energy technologies.

In 1982 the company entered a new field when it took on its first large government defense contract to create a survivable base for the MX missile system. The firm is also helping large manufacturers to develop cogeneration facilities, waste heat-recovery systems, and solid waste energy-production systems.

Some of the far-flung activities and innovative applications of new technologies being accomplished by Gilbert/Commonwealth may seem unusual for a relatively small local firm, but they follow in the tradition that was laid down by its founders. The firm's achievements today in far-off places are comparable to the challenges of constructing major new electric generating facilities along the Kalamazoo River in the early 1890s and on the Manistee and AuSable rivers within the next few years.

It was J.B. Foote and William C.

These drafting tables were the work place for company engineers in the 1940s and 1950s.

Fargo who formed a partnership and set out to develop power on the Kalamazoo River and transmit it to the growing community of Kalamazoo, a then-incredible 25 miles upstream. Foote was the younger brother of W.A. Foote, who is credited with establishing Jackson-based Consumers Power Company and for whom Foote Memorial Hospital is named.

The pair of engineers reached another milestone when they sought to harness the power of more northern rivers from which electricity had to be transmitted farther to get to population centers. In 1912 they developed a transmission line capable of carrying power at 140,000 volts, a previously unheard-of level. Among the delegations that journeyed to Michigan from around the world to marvel at the new high-voltage line was one headed by the wizard of electrical research, Charles Steinmetz, who commented in awe, "to think, it has never been done before."

The developments which led to what became Commonwealth Associates Inc. began about 1910, when electric light and power companies in Michigan, Ohio, Illinois, and Indiana were joined into an organization called The Commonwealth Power, Railway and Light Company. Over the next 20 years the scope of work of the engineering group of this organization expanded greatly, taking on more and more projects for the affiliated companies and developing a number of innovations in the electric industry.

A series of public utility consolidations culminated in the 1929 incorporation of The Commonwealth and Southern Corporation, a billion-dollar holding company. It included not only electric utilities, but gas-manufacturing companies, steam-heating plants, water-pumping stations, street railways, bus companies, an electric interurban system, coal mines, and even an amusement park.

While most of the management consulting personnel of the conglomerate's service arm were located in New York City, the department, which handled the general engineering for the northern group of member firms, was located in Jackson. It primarily provided services to Consumers Power Company and to other present-day firms such as Central Illinois Light Company, Southern Indiana Gas and Electric Company, Ohio Edison Company, and Pennsylvania Power Company.

During the two decades of its existence, Commonwealth and Southern was regarded as a model system, characterized by efficient management and operation. However, the financial misfortunes of other utility holding companies, principally those afflicting the conglomerate of Samuel Insull in

Chicago, cast their cloud over C&S and other economically stable systems. In 1935 the newly passed Public Utility Holding Company Act mandated the dissolution of Commonwealth and Southern along with many other such firms.

One of the last acts in the dissolution was the formation of Commonwealth Services, Inc., of New York on October 7, 1949, as an independent engineering and management consulting services company. At the same time, its subsidiary engineering organization, Commonwealth Associates Inc., was established. Some 95 percent of the entire Commonwealth group's staff was with the Jackson subsidiary.

In the period following the formation of Commonwealth Services, Inc., the utility companies with which it had been formerly affiliated were its principal clients. Soon, however, the organization was expanded to a management services subsidiary and a transportation consulting arm.

In 1970 Commonwealth Services, Inc., merged with Computer Sciences Corporation of California, a firm specializing in information technology and computer software.

In 1973 Commonwealth was acquired by Gilbert Associates, Inc., of Reading, Pennsylvania, which has similar expertise as an international engineering consulting firm. Gilbert had a similar history of once having been the engineering arm of a major utility holding company, Associated Gas & Electric, that was broken up as a result of the Public Utility Holding Company Act. At its inception, the 200 Gilbert employees bought the company. By the time of the 1973 merger with Common-

wealth Services, Gilbert had grown to 1,600 employees. Today the entire Gilbert organization has about 4,000 employees.

The current location of Gilbert/Commonwealth is 209 East Washington Avenue in Jackson.

The headquarters of Commonwealth Power Co., the engineering arm of which became Commonwealth Associates Inc., was located at Michigan Avenue and Hayes Street. Photo courtesy of Consumers Power Company.

JACKSON STORES INC.

In 1869, as downtown Jackson was being improved with flagstone walkways, Abram Jacobson was opening a small women's apparel shop far to the north, in downtown Reed City, which lies along the ring finger of Michigan's mittened hand.

That first Jacobson's was the predecessor of what is now a chain of 19 stores across Michigan, Ohio, and Florida. The company, purchased by the Rosenfeld family in 1939, went public in 1972. The name Jacobson's is synonymous with current fashion and high quality.

Moses L. Jacobson, who succeeded his father as president of the fledgling enterprise, traveled around the state, showing fashions and making sales from the eight or 10 trunks he carried. He eventually moved to Jackson, and with his brother, William, purchased the Faulkner-Porter Store in 1904, a 15-by 80-foot shop at 105 East Main Street. In 1918 the Jacobsons built a new building farther along the renamed street, at 113 Michigan.

The company grew, was incorporated, and opened stores in other cities. When Moses died in 1930, his brother continued operation of the business, but sold it in 1939 to Nathan Rosenfeld and his brother, Zola. At that time the firm employed 45 people in its three stores in Jackson, Ann Arbor, and Battle Creek.

Nathan Rosenfeld closed the deal to purchase Jacobson's on a Friday afternoon. Immediately afterward the store's manager, Richard Jacobson, William's son, left for a weekend trip. Unfortunately, he took with him the combination to the store's fur vault. A major fur sale was to begin the next morning. When Rosenfeld learned that both the furs and Richard were unreachable, he thought quickly and called a new Jackson acquaintance, the prison warden. Two nimble-fingered convicts were volunteered. Rosenfeld liked to recall that they came into town with a guard and had the vault's lock opened in a matter of minutes. They were rewarded with a pitcher of beer.

Under the Rosenfelds' direction, the stores have grown in number, expanded in size, and prospered. A central office, at 1200 North West Avenue, was opened in 1949. It contained the first example in American retailing, outside of New York City, of central receipt, ticketing, and distribution of fashion merchandise.

Jacobson's hometown store moved farther down the street again—to 255 West Michigan. The enlarged establishment opened in 1961 and combined women's, men's, and children's clothing. Around the corner, at 280 West Cortland Street, is Jacobson's Store for the Home, which carries furniture, home furnishings, and related accessories.

When the concern began acquiring stores in Florida, it first operated them under the names "Yankee Traveler" and "Proctor's."

Those stores are now also called Jacobson's and have a central distribution office in Florida.

Zola Rosenfeld died in 1961, and Nathan Rosenfeld, former chairman of the board and prime mover of the company, died in 1982. J. Russell Fowler, a Jackson native, joined the company in 1945, was named president in 1966, and became chairman in 1982. Nathan's son, Mark, is now president of the firm.

It was Nathan Rosenfeld, who, with Russ Fowler, his protégé, played an important role in developing downtown Jackson and set the tone for the enterprise. It is reflected in Jacobson's store motto, created in 1949: *Si labor tibi faciendus est, hic est bonus locus.* Translated, it means: "If you have to work, this is a good place to be."

Nathan Rosenfeld, former Jacobson's chairman of the board, inspired the firm's motto: Si labor tibi faciendus est, hic est bonus locus, *meaning "If you have to work, this is a good place to be." Courtesy of the Jackson Citizen Patriot.*

Moses Jacobson constructed the Esther Jacobson Building at 113 Michigan Avenue in 1918. As his business grew he acquired adjacent stores to enlarge the apparel store.

WILLBEE CONCRETE PRODUCTS & WILLBEE TRANSIT MIX COMPANY, INC.

Since they deal in concrete and cement, both Willbee Concrete Products and Willbee Transit Mix Company can be said to be built on a solid foundation. That foundation, however, is based on more than its products. The two enterprises have behind them a tradition of family strength and sound business growth.

The firm was begun in 1907 in Adrian by Charles H. Willbee and his twin brother, Frank. The fledgling venture's principal products were burial vaults, and its biggest market was Jackson, which meant that vaults had to be transported by horse and wagon or sleigh, depending on the season. Business was so good that a Jackson plant was established in 1911, and both were maintained until 1922 when the Adrian plant was sold.

In Jackson, Charles E. Willbee, who succeeded his father, added concrete blocks to the company's product line. The first blocks were handmade. The cement was mixed manually, scooped with a shovel, and poured into small individual molds. A standard block measured 8 by 8 by 24 inches and weighed 55 pounds.

By 1930 cement blocks were made on a huge high-powered Besser Block Machine capable of turning out 40 different types of blocks at the rate of 4,000 per day. By the late 1930s burial vaults comprised about 50 percent of production and blocks the remaining 50 percent.

Charles W. Willbee and Richard S. Willbee, the sons of Charles E., had joined Willbee Concrete in 1947 and founded Willbee Transit Mix in 1954 to meet the changing needs of the concrete industry. Though cement blocks were still a large part of their business (a new machine was able to produce 1,000 blocks an hour), construction practices were changing.

Ready-mixed concrete was used more in road and bridge construction, and it was required to be more precise in its makeup. Willbee Transit Mix installed a $25,000, completely automatic concrete mixing plant—the first of its kind in Michigan—in response to quality-control requirements of the Michigan Highway Department and other contractors. The new electronically controlled system helped increase production by about 30 percent.

In 1973 Willbee Concrete Products Company moved from its former location, 215 West Euclid, to a new facility at 2323 Brooklyn Road, after spending $800,000 for new buildings and equipment. It was joined a few years later by Willbee Transit Mix Company, which built a new concrete batch plant and offices on the 9.5-acre site.

Management of the two firms has always stayed in the family—when Charles E. retired in 1971, sons Charles W. and Richard S. Willbee took over the business. To accommodate the next generation of Willbees, the companies were divided in 1978 so that Charles and his son became the only stockholders of Willbee Concrete Products, and Richard and his sons became the only stockholders of Willbee Transit Mix Company.

Willbee Concrete Products is engaged in the production and wholesale sales of Wilbert Burial Vaults and other burial products, and in cremation services that were recently installed. The firm also produces and distributes "Min-it-Mix" concrete and mortar and similar products in 80- and 50-pound bags, used mostly for repair and for small new building projects.

Willbee Transit Mix delivers mixed concrete from its modern, state-approved plant with a fleet of 10 new front-discharge mixer trucks. It also supplies concrete blocks and special building supplies related to construction needs.

Each company has sales of close to two million dollars annually. Together they employ about 40 people during heavy work periods.

Willbee Concrete Products and Willbee Transit Mix Company share a 9.5-acre site at 2323 Brooklyn Road.

R.A. GREENE WASTEWATER TREATMENT PLANT

As a city grows in population and industry, the way it treats its wastes is a factor in the quality of life it has to offer. In some cities, wastewater treatment is not always an efficient process, but is often an expensive one.

Part of what Jackson has to offer its people and those who would consider locating here is an up-to-date facility that does its job at a far lower cost than in many other Michigan communities. According to a 1984 study, the average bill for residential sewer service in 14 Michigan cities was about $26.85 quarterly. At the same time, Jackson's rate was $9.02. Commercial and industrial rates were also correspondingly lower. A three-year plan to make Jackson's sewage treatment plant self-sufficient contains projected rates that still are well below the Michigan average.

In addition to those low rates, the wastewater treatment system can handle new and expanded use far into the future. It has the capacity to treat about 19 million gallons of wastewater daily, and in the mid-1980s is using only about two-thirds of its capacity.

Jackson's residents can thank their city officials who, since the 1930s, have had the foresight to fund the

The plant's aeration and final settling tanks are part of the process that purifies Jackson's wastewater.

installation and expansion of wastewater treatment facilities to meet both present and future needs. The heart of the system is the R.A. Greene Wastewater Treatment Plant, located at 2995 Lansing Avenue. The system serves the city of Jackson; the townships of Summit, Spring Arbor, Napoleon, and Blackman; and Southern Michigan Prison.

Hidden from view, the plant straddles the Grand River at the back of the R.A. Greene Park. It takes sewage from homes and businesses and turns it into water clean enough to be discharged into the river.

After mechanical removal of materials such as rags and grit, sewage goes through primary treatment (removal of matter that settles) and secondary treatment (the biological process which uses microorganisms to metabolize soluble

matter in the water). Further chemical treatment results in clean, chlorinated water, and in sludge which is used by farmers in place of commercial fertilizer because of the nutrients it provides to the soil.

When wastewater treatment facilities were built in 1935, the plant could handle a volume of six million gallons per day. The most recent expansion, completed in 1981, also resolved a decades-old problem for the community. The area's sewer system had carried both rainwater and sanitary sewage. As a result, the wastewater treatment plant was forced to process excess volumes of wastewater, and during heavy rains the sewers became so overloaded that raw sewage would be dumped into the river.

The problem was solved through Jackson's largest public works project ever. The city separated the sewer system into storm and sanitary components. Some 46 miles of sewers were installed at a cost of $27.9 million, 75 percent of which was funded by the state and federal governments. The project's completion has resulted in a cleaner Grand River and a more efficient, economical wastewater treatment system.

An aerial view of the R. A. Green Wastewater Treatment Plant.

CITY OF JACKSON WATER DEPARTMENT

Water. Without it, life cannot exist. And without abundant, clean, and inexpensive water, modern-day cities and the industries that form their financial base cannot survive.

Jackson has a plentiful supply of clean water. More than three billion gallons a year are pumped from the city's 12 deep wells and piped to 13,000 customers in the city of Jackson and portions of Blackman, Leoni, and Summit townships. Under the direction of superintendent Lawrence E. Everett and the city water department, a reliable supply of clean, treated water will be available to Jackson residents and businesses for as long as planners can project.

It was in 1870 that the city of Jackson chartered a water service by issuing $100,000 in capital stock to form the Jackson City Water Company. The growing city was far past the stage of having one town pump, and needed deeper wells and a distribution system to supply its increasing population. Five miles of glazed iron pipe and a "substantial brick engine house" were called for in the original plans.

The water department began business with a small pump capable of pumping 1.5 million gallons a

In 1977 the city built this plant on East Mansion Street to soften and treat city water.

day. Water rates were based on the number of people and fixtures in a structure. For example, a boarding house was charged $1.25 a year for each room in the house; one-family dwellings were charged $5 for one faucet and $2 for each additional faucet.

The city completed its pumping station on Water Street in 1885 and drilled additional wells up to 390 feet deep on that site by 1890. A gigantic—by 1885 standards— Holly-Gaskill pump, which could pump four million gallons a day, was added and expected to meet the community's needs for years to come.

A reservoir was added to the Water Street complex in 1916 to provide water for fighting fires; previously, water had been pumped from the river.

In 1917 the city drilled new wells on Mansion Street. That well field today is the heart of the water department—pumps were transferred there and only one standby well remains with the department's office and garage on Water Street. New, high-capacity pumps were added to the growing Mansion Street facility. By the water department's 50th anniversary, the city boasted more than 100 miles of completed water mains, almost 11,000 meters in use, and water revenues approaching $200,000.

The Water Street pumping station, built in 1885, was the first major component in Jackson's Water Department.

Jackson's residents have cleaner, softer water since the city's water treatment facility was built in 1977. The $6.8-million facility can purify up to 24 million gallons of water daily, taking out about 75 percent of the hardness and removing all the iron. On an average day, the treatment plant uses about 140 pounds of ferric chloride, 10 tons of lime, 1.7 tons of soda ash, and 270 pounds of fluoride to purify and improve the water.

Now, in the mid-1980s, water is pumped from Jackson's 12 wells, through the water treatment plant, and into a 7.5-million-gallon storage reservoir on Mansion Street or into one of two elevated 1.5-million-gallon tanks on Tyson Street and North West Avenue. It is then distributed to customers through 200 miles of water mains and to 1,700 hydrants in the area. Water Department revenues in 1983 totaled three million dollars, which for an average residential customer meant just over $25 for household water used in a three-month period.

CONSUMERS POWER COMPANY

W.A. Foote, founder of Consumers Power Company. Photo circa 1910.

The corporate history of Consumers Power Company is titled "Future Builders," and employees of the firm have long taken pride in the fact that their company has played a vital role in building both Jackson's and Michigan's future. Growth and innovation have been hallmarks in the history of the utility, which marks its 100th anniversary in 1986.

The long list of utility industry precedents that contributed to Michigan's growth began in the company's early days and continues today. For example, in 1908 the Croton Hydroelectric Dam—still in operation—began operating on the Muskegon River, and its transmission line carried electricity at 110,000 volts, an unprecedented electric pressure that required innovative new porcelain insulators to keep the line from burning out. When word spread that the Michigan utility was transmitting power at 100,000-plus volts, distinguished engineers from around the world came to Jackson and Grand Rapids to learn more about

this pacesetting achievement.

The Cooke Dam on the AuSable River, completed in 1911, brought a new breakthrough in the electric utility business. The power was transmitted through Saginaw and Bay City into Flint, Zilwaukee, and

Owosso, a distance of 151 miles, greater than had ever been

Consumers Power Company's headquarters in 1936 (below) and today (bottom). The building, erected in 1927, received a face-lift in the late 1960s.

attempted before. To overcome this challenge, the pressure was stepped up to 140,000 volts, a level that had never before been achieved.

Consumers Power was one of the first utilities to see the need for, and value in, rural electrification. In 1949 it became the first utility in the country to serve more than 100,000 farm customers.

Realizing early on the potential of nuclear energy, the company was among the pioneers in the burgeoning industry with the development of the Big Rock Point nuclear plant, which was Michigan's first, and the nation's fifth, commercial nuclear reactor when it went into operation in December 1962. The plant is the oldest boiling-water reactor in the world still in service. In 1983 the facility was subjected to a major in-service inspection which assessed the physical and mechanical systems, including various safety systems and the reactor vessel itself. In virtually all cases the diagnosis was that the plant is in excellent shape.

Consumers Power was the first utility in the country to develop plans for a nuclear-powered co-generation facility. The Midland nuclear plant, announced in 1967, was intended to generate electricity and produce steam to be used for manufacturing by the Dow Chemical Company. Dow has withdrawn from participation in the project because of delays in completing the plant, but Consumers Power designers and engineers take pride in their innovative development of the nuclear co-generation concept.

While the Ludington pumped storage hydroelectric plant was not the first such facility when it was completed in 1973, it was, and remains, the world's largest. Cited by the American Society of Civil Engineers as the outstanding civil

engineering achievement of 1973, the plant serves as a "giant storage battery" for its joint owners, Consumers Power and the Detroit Edison Company. While a typical power plant may require hours or even days to reach full power from a cold start, Ludington can be at full power on one of its six 312,000-megawatt hydroelectric generators in three to four minutes. All six units can be at full power within 30 minutes.

The Marysville natural gas reforming plant, expanding a concept that was developed in Great Britain in the 1920s, was the nation's first, and possibly the world's largest, such facility when it began operation in 1973. The plant used a refining process to transform natural gas liquids into natural gas of the same quality as that produced through natural gas drilling. During severe winters in the mid-1970s, when gas shortages developed in other states forcing the closure of schools, factories, and commercial businesses, Marysville's production helped stave off similar closings in Michigan. The plant has been moth-balled since 1979, but is expected to be needed again beginning in the late 1980s.

Consumers Power's wholly owned oil and gas exploration and development subsidiary, Northern Michigan Exploration Company (NOMECO), was one of the nation's first such utility subsidiaries when it was established in 1969. It has also been one of the most successful. NOMECO has a debt-free balance sheet and is able to support a multimillion-dollar exploration program entirely with internal funding. In addition to conducting operations in the southwestern United States and the Gulf of Mexico, NOMECO has interests in Australia, Canada, Colombia, Tonga, and Belize.

Anticipating an eventual downturn in the availability of uranium for nuclear plants, the company purchased a uranium development firm and created its own uranium subsidiary, Plateau Resources, Ltd., in 1975. Its $142 million in assets at the end of 1983 included a uranium mill in southeastern Utah with a demonstrated capacity of one

Consumers Power, by the time of this 1905 photo, had been powering electric streetcars in the Jackson area for 15 years.

Consumers Power Company has always promoted the city's growth, as shown by this photo of the firm's No. 1 wagon.

million pounds of uranium concentrates per year, and extensive mining properties in southeastern Utah and southwestern Colorado.

Consumers Power is and has been prominent in Jackson and environs. In 1983 approximately 4,000 of its 12,000-plus employees were working in its Jackson headquarters and its district offices. For decades it has been the largest employer in Jackson County.

During the years the company has been in operation, many men and women have made contributions to its development. The first—and perhaps the foremost—was W.A. Foote, a native of Adrian who came to Jackson in 1886. The 32-year-old Foote obtained approval from the Jackson Common Council to demonstrate electric arc lights to illuminate downtown streets. "There is no reason why this city should lag behind the other great and growing cities of this state," said Foote in petitioning the council members.

The demonstration was successful and Foote was awarded a franchise. He established the Jackson Electric Light Works, the city's predecessor to today's Consumers Power Company. For many years the enterprise was located in a setback

building facing Mechanic Street near the corner of Trail.

Foote also established electric light firms in Battle Creek and Albion, and later bought an existing electric utility in Kalamazoo. It was during this period, the late 19th and early 20th centuries, that he conceived the idea of a statewide interconnected electric system. During the same period two financiers, Anton G. Hodenpyl of Grand Rapids and Henry D.W. Walbridge of Kalamazoo, were consolidating various gas companies, including one in Jackson, under the umbrella of the Michigan Light Company. It was only natural that the entrepreneurs combine forces, and in 1910 they established Consumers Power Company.

The firm's development followed the route of Michigan's growth— and in many instances powered that growth—into a major industrial state. In 1921 the company had 130,000 electric and 60,000 gas customers. By 1940 electric users numbered 467,000 and gas customers totaled 209,000. The biggest expansion came during the postwar years. Between 1950 and 1975 the number of electric customers increased by 80 percent and the number of gas customers by 107 percent.

In the mid-1980s Consumers Power was one of only four combination gas and electric utilities in the nation to serve more than

one million electric customers and one million gas customers. About 435,000 of these were both electric and gas customers at the end of 1983.

The firm's service area encompasses 31,535 square miles. Included are such metropolitan centers as suburban Detroit, Lansing, Kalamazoo, Grand Rapids, Flint, Pontiac, Muskegon, Saginaw, Bay City, Battle Creek, and, of course, Jackson. Consumers Power also continues to serve large rural areas—more than 49,000 farms are customers. Industries in the territory served by Consumers Power include automobiles, primary metals, chemicals, metal fabricating, oil refining, pharmaceuticals, machinery, paper and paper products, food processing, and others.

The enterprise has eight operating regions, each supervised by a general manager responsible for engineering, construction, operation, and maintenance of electric and gas distribution systems, energy consulting services, accounting, customer services, and employee and public affairs. About 6,000 employees are located in the regions;

The Ludington pumped storage hydroelectric plant, the largest facility of its type in the world, can generate 1.8 million kilowatts of electricity within minutes. It is owned jointly by Consumers Power and the Detroit Edison Company.

4,000 work in the engineering, electric and gas supply, customer service, accounting, and other departments in the corporate headquarters; and approximately 2,000 are involved in the company's 5 fossil, 7 combustion turbine, 14 hydroelectric, and 2 operating nuclear plants.

The newest coal-fired unit, J.H. Campbell 3, named after a former president of Consumers Power, went into service in September 1980. Should one of the units of the mothballed Midland nuclear plant be placed in operation, the company will rely on coal for approximately 66 percent of its internally generated electric production, on nuclear power for approximately 32 percent, on oil and gas for about .5 percent, and on hydro for 1.5 percent. Until the 1940s most gas sold by utilities was manufactured from coal or coke. In fact, the first manufactured gas plant in Jackson predated W.A. Foote's electric company by nearly 30 years. In 1857 Edward Coen was granted permission by the newly incorporated city of Jackson to build a coal-gas plant which was built on the west side of Mechanic Street, between Luther Street (now Pearl Street) and the Grand River.

Manufactured gas had a low heat content and was used primarily for illumination, although a method utilizing steam during the manufacturing process did produce a gas of sufficient warmth to be used for home heating. The 1940s saw a tremendous increase in available supplies of natural gas from the Southwest and led Consumers Power to eventually shut down its manufactured gas operations.

Through its subsidiaries, the Michigan Gas Storage Company and NOMECO, Consumers Power receives gas from Texas, Oklahoma, Louisiana, and the Gulf of Mexico,

as well as from fields in central and northern Michigan. The sources of gas are supported by 14 natural gas storage fields operated by Consumers Power and Michigan Gas Storage. On peak cold days as much as 70 percent of the gas sold by the firm is supplied from these storage fields.

Other subsidiaries wholly owned by Consumers Power are Michigan Utility Collection Service Co., Inc., which is engaged in a special collection service for past-due utility service bills, and Utility Systems, Inc., which coordinates information about construction work or other activities that might take place in areas where electric and gas lines are located. Another subsidiary, Consumers Power Finance, N.V., was organized in the Netherlands Antilles in 1973. Its purpose is to obtain financing from sources outside the United States to support activities of the company and its subsidiaries.

Consumers Power looks forward to its second century with a positive outlook, based in part on projections by the U.S. Department of Energy that indicate the Midwest should benefit from reliable supplies of electricity at relatively stable prices for the remainder of this century. The DOE says that utilities in the region are sensibly basing future electric supplies on coal and, in particular, the atom. By contrast, electric companies in the Sun Belt states are relying heavily on oil and

The J.H. Campbell Unit 3, named after a former president of the company, is the newest coal-fired electric generating plant owned by Consumers Power.

natural gas, both very expensive by comparison to coal and uranium, as electric generating fuels. The department believes that could lead to soaring costs and electricity shortages.

"The contrast in outlook for the two regions is unlikely to be lost on U.S. businessmen planning to expand or relocate facilities," says John D. Selby, chairman of the board of Consumers Power Company. "It provides yet another reason for optimism regarding Michigan's economic future."

The Big Rock Point nuclear plant, located near Charlevoix, was Michigan's first, and the nation's fifth, such facility when it began operating in 1962.

MICHIGAN INTERNATIONAL SPEEDWAY

For an institution that wasn't originally intended to be located in Jackson, the Michigan International Speedway certainly has made a tremendous contribution to the area. With more than 250,000 people attending events at MIS, area officials estimate that the annual racing programs and other activities inject millions of dollars into the area's economy.

Jackson citizens who benefit from MIS activities can thank the people of Saline. Back in 1966 when Detroit entrepreneur Lawrence H. Lopatin began efforts to implement a long-held dream of Michigan automobile buffs—a quality racetrack for the state whose name is synonymous with auto production—he selected a site in Washtenaw County, south of I-94 near Saline.

When the announcement appeared, area residents turned, in the words of one reporter, "violent." They jammed a zoning board meeting, and Lopatin called it one of the worst nights of his life. He

Two Indy Car drivers, who are part of the Penske racing team, are Al Unser, Sr., 1983 CART/PPG Indy Car champion, in car No. 7, and Rick Mears, 1982 Indy Car champion, in car No. 1.

Roger S. Penske bid $2.9 million in bankruptcy court and came away the new owner of Michigan International Speedway.

walked out and began looking further. In early 1967 Lopatin found 800 acres of gentle rolling farmland and wood lots in the Irish Hills, north and west of Cambridge Junction where U.S. 12 and M-50 cross.

Having learned his lesson, Lopatin moved cautiously. Only after he found that he had broad community support did he firm up his plans. Lopatin promised the new track would "be the yardstick by which every other (race) circuit in the world will be gauged."

Ground was broken for the eventual $5-million speedway on September 27, 1967. Celebrities included Stirling Moss, renowned British racing driver, and Henry Banks, director of competition for the U.S. Auto Club. The architect was Charles Moneypenny, who designed the famous Daytona

(Florida) Speedway.

MIS was designed to be the world's most complete racing plant. It is easily accessible to more than 10 million people within a radius of 175 miles. Its tracks provide a banked, D-shaped, two-mile oval for high-speed racing of all types of cars, a road course of 2.75 miles inside and outside the main oval, and two road courses of about 1.75 miles each with the curves that make up this type of racing, but have remained unused since 1972. A new 1.9-mile infield road course was completed in late 1983, utilizing existing paved surfaces. It will debut in September 1984 with an IMSA road race.

Virtually all parts of these courses are visible from the main grandstand, an advantage few racecourses have. The race control tower, garages, and facilities for the media are probably the finest in the country. Ample parking is provided on the property.

A 250-mile Indy Car event was to inaugurate MIS. However, Jackson-area businessmen were somewhat

This 1981 aerial photo of Michigan International Speedway shows its interior road course, changed slightly since then, and part of its exterior road course.

underwhelmed with the developing raceway. In a March 1968 speech to 112 members of the Greater Jackson Chamber of Commerce, Lopatin urged them to "get involved" in his project. "You're sitting back and saying 'the thing won't fly,'" he said.

Whether at Lopatin's urging or by the realization of MIS' potential, Jackson-area businesses did get involved. Pre-inaugural race events included a display of cars with drivers and equipment in Jackson-area shopping malls, publication of an inaugural edition by the *Jackson Citizen Patriot*, distribution of 25,000 placemats to area restaurants, publication of a directory of area auto repair and material supply locations, special buses from downtown Jackson to the race, and helicopter service from the city's downtown urban-renewal area to the infield of MIS.

More than 55,000 spectators viewed the inaugural event. Michigan Governor George

Romney, who previously had headed American Motors, took the wheel of the pace car the day before the race.

From that first event to this day, drivers have called the course the fastest Indy Car track in the country. In fact, in September 1983 champion Rick Mears won the Detroit News Grand Prix with an average speed of 182.325 miles an hour, the fastest Indy Car average race speed in history.

In its brief history MIS has developed a reputation for innovation. In 1970 it launched twin 200s, conducting races featuring Indy cars and a separate event with stock cars. That concept continues in an expanded fashion today at MIS with the addition of "Super Vees" in the Detroit News Grand Prix triple-header each September.

Also in 1970 the 400-mile distance for NASCAR's two races was begun. It continued each year with the Miller High Life 400 in June and the Champion Spark Plug 400 in August. The only other 400-miler is the Firecracker 400 at Daytona. In spite of its success and innovation, MIS' owners had problems. In 1972 its parent company, American Raceways, went into receivership under a formula that allowed the track to maintain its racing schedule. The financial problems were not with MIS—its 1972 racing schedule produced a profit of $250,000. However, Lopatin had overreached himself in trying to establish a chain of racetracks around the country.

Fortunately a savior emerged in the form of Roger Penske, former champion driver and successful businessman, who, with his Penske Corporation, purchased MIS for $2.9 million. He then began an innovative plan to improve the track and make it one of the country's finest racing complexes.

Among the improvements instituted by Penske was the addition of 8,000 seats, bringing total seating to 33,000; the rebuilding of the scoring stand structure; paving of the garage and

Few racetracks are wide enough to accommodate five cars abreast, one reason Michigan International Speedway is known as a safe track.

participant parking areas; new concession and restroom facilities; new maintenance equipment; and the addition of a jet-powered track drier. In 1977 the entire oval was resurfaced under the supervison of Clarence Cagle, retired superintendent of the Indianapolis Motor Speedway. In the spring of 1982 a $300,000 concrete barrier that stretches through the turns at both ends of the track was completed.

Penske's improvement program reached a temporary peak in 1982—he plans more improvements in the future—with the completion of the terrace suite communications complex, which features eight new luxury viewing suites, new press facilities, and offices for MIS vice-president and general manager Darwin Doll and his staff. Since 1977 Penske has earmarked more than one million dollars for improvements.

Penske has also helped develop a number of improvements in the competitive arena. In 1974 he was a leader in the development of the International Race of Champions series. That program uses identically prepared vehicles—in its early days Porsches, now Camaros—in sprint events with the world's finest drivers.

Cale Yarborough's front tire smokes during a fast pit stop for refueling, new tires, and cleanup during a NASCAR race for Grand National stock cars.

In 1981 he announced the inaugural Norton-Michigan 500, making MIS only the sixth track to run a 500-mile Indy Car race. The year 1981 also saw the American Speed Association Circuit of Champions cars make their first appearance at MIS.

Shortly after Penske's takeover, an agreement was concluded that helped cement MIS' economic stability. In July 1973 American Motors Corporation made MIS its principal testing facility, primarily to test emission-control equipment. The testing program operates 24 hours a day, approximately 340 days a year. Nearly 90 percent of the testing involves exhaust systems designed to help the AMC vehicles meet Environmental Protection Agency certification requirements.

The remaining 10 percent of the program involves general development, including fuel economy, body corrosion, vehicle noise, and drive-line development. There are an average of 15 cars on the high-banked oval track at all times. All late-model AMC products are tested for a 50,000-mile duration with in-depth inspections every 5,000 miles.

More than 100 drivers, most of them local housewives, participate in the testing. Since the program began in 1973, more than 20 million miles had been driven in the first 10 years of the test effort. Because of the AMC testing program, Michigan International Speedway gets several hundred times more use than any other track in the country.

Another significant test program takes place each autumn. The exterior racecourse becomes the scene for the annual Michigan State Police test of U.S. car models to select the vehicle best suited for a patrol car. About a dozen automobiles are tested each year.

Police agencies from across the country have relied on the tests at MIS for their patrol car purchases. Michigan officials distribute more than 800 copies of their findings each year, and the International Association of Police Chiefs reprints as many as 8,000 copies.

Apart from the obvious contributions that MIS makes to the Jackson-area economy, the speedway helps provide other benefits to the community. The annual golf outing held each July in connection with the Michigan 500 had, by 1983, contributed nearly $60,000 to Foote Memorial Hospital. An MIS-sponsored roast of champion driver Tom Sneva helped raise money for the International Guiding Eyes, a nonprofit organization providing trained guide dogs for the blind. And, in a continuing program that helps area service organizations, MIS uses members of such groups as the Boy Scouts of America and area service clubs as workers.

The people of Saline have certainly made a long-lasting contribution to the Jackson area, and the creative innovations of the Roger Penske organization have helped to firm up the Michigan International Speedway—a Jackson institution.

In 1982 a $300,000 concrete barrier was constructed along the turns at both ends of the track.

ADCO PRODUCTS, INC.

Although many Jackson industries have existed for decades, helping to form the foundation of the community's economic strength, without new, successful businesses being established over the years, that strength would begin to erode. One of those new firms, ADCO Products, Inc., has made significant contributions to the area's economy, especially during the difficult economic times of the early 1980s.

Consider that ADCO's sales rose from $250,000 in 1972, when it began production, to a projected $12 million in 1984. And consider that its work force increased from just a few employees that first year to more than 100 in early 1984. Top it off with a planned expansion, funded with industrial revenue bonds underwritten by the Jackson County Economic Development

Corporation that will add 15,000 square feet of production and additional employment, and you can see that ADCO is well on its way to becoming an old-line Jackson business.

Like many enterprises, however, ADCO almost didn't make it. President Charles O. Pyron said the first year of business was so tough that "we almost went broke." In fact, it wasn't until 1974 that the firm made a profit.

ADCO is a manufacturer of adhesives and moldings for the automotive and marine industries. It also produces material to caulk windows and mobile homes and to seal underground pipes. In addition, ADCO provides custom mixing and formulating services to other sealant manufacturers. Its location at 4401 Page Avenue, Michigan Center, close to Route 127 and Interstate 94, makes it ideally situated to serve customers from the East Coast to the Rockies.

The company's growth, in recent years, is primarily attributable to its sales to the auto industry. ADCO sells adhesives for car trim to General Motors Corporation and supplies GM component manufacturers with adhesives for taillight and windshield moldings. The firm also does some business with Ford Motor Company.

While the automotive industry has been good to ADCO, the firm is dealing with other industries, as well. "We're fortunate in that we have developed new products that are sold to a variety of markets," Pyron says. He notes that the company has flourished because it has "a good staff and carries on a strong development program."

Like many earlier Jackson industrialists, Pyron and his executive vice-president, Donald R. Strack, migrated to this community to make their mark. Both were

engineers and executives of a Dayton, Ohio, adhesives firm and both wanted to run their own organization.

Why Jackson? In addition to its ideal location, the plant site, which had previously been used for a sealant-production operation, was available at a reasonable price. At first the plant was much too large for their needs. Production utilized only 20,000 square feet of the 80,000-square-foot building. However, by 1978 the firm was planning to double its existing warehouse space. In 1981 ADCO Products, Inc., utilized an economic development bond to expand to its present capacity of 110,000 square feet. And the planned expansion can only bode well for the future. All in all, not a bad growth record for a Jackson-area company that in the mid-1980s is barely into its teens.

Charles O. Pyron, president of ADCO Products, Inc.

Donald R. Strack, executive vice-president.

JACKSON OSTEOPATHIC HOSPITAL

Jackson Osteopathic Hospital noted its 40th anniversary in 1984 with the dedication of its enlarged, completely remodeled facility, up-to-date equipment, and the beginning of two important new programs—its Doctors Care Center and a cooperative internship program.

The hospital has remained small due to health planning restrictions, but the organization reflects a strength that comes from its private corporate structure of 50 medical staff members and private citizens. It is that core of support that has allowed the hospital, through its own efforts, to finance its modernization over the years.

Jackson Osteopathic was incorporated in the summer of 1943 by five osteopathic physicians, Drs. John D. Root, Leslie B. Walker, Donald W. Brail, Alan R. Becker, and W. Powell Cottrille. Drs. Root and Walker mortgaged their own homes to buy the Morey mansion at 121 Seymour, a large house that boasted multiple fireplaces and a ballroom. There were 12 beds and 5 bassinets in the new hospital, but no elevator, so patients were carried up and down stairs on litters.

The facility began as a general hospital, handling all types of cases including obstetrics and surgery. Dr. Root was the institution's only surgeon during its first 20 years of existence. It was Dr. Root who provided much of the equipment for the new hospital. He had operated an eight-bed facility in Leslie for five years before his move to Jackson.

In the early days, nurses worked 12-hour shifts, and the doctors' wives helped with the cooking and with sewing and mending. Keeping the hospital afloat was difficult during the first seven or eight years. At one point each staff member was required to contribute $500 to cover overhead and to ward off insolvency. Today the hospital has just completed a $5.5-million expansion and renovation.

During its first 20 years the hospital charged its practicing physicians a daily "bed assessment" fee for each of the doctor's hospitalized patients. Not an uncommon practice among small, private hospitals before the advent of widespread health insurance, the fee was $7.50 for minor surgery, medical, and obstetrics patients and $15 for major surgery care.

The facility's patient load grew steadily, and the corporation added on to the Morey home a number of times before it was finally torn down and a new structure erected in its place. A major expansion in 1956 added 3,000 square feet, and another 10,000 square feet were added in 1964. By then, hospital planners had developed a five-stage master plan for growth based on a lengthy study involving community surveys and private consultants' work.

In 1969 the hospital more than doubled in size with a million-dollar expansion. A new three-story, 20,000-square-foot addition included many ancillary services—emergency, obstetrics, surgery, laboratories, pharmacy, and radiology—as well as other patient care areas. At that point, the hospital's bed count stood at 50 and its annual patient days at just over 14,000.

Health care planning became an issue in the mid-1970s, when comprehensive studies were undertaken to project future needs for medical facilities. Jackson Osteopathic Hospital, which then had 75 beds, changed its plans for further growth. Instead of adding new beds, hospital officials decided to improve services like laboratory, X-ray, and outpatient care. Health care planning also prompted the consolidation of emergency room and obstetrical services in Jackson—both were located at Foote Memorial Hospital, the community's larger facility.

Still needing space for its growing patient load, in 1979 Osteopathic Hospital announced a multimillion-dollar program of addition and renovation. It would maintain its number of beds at 75, as limited by regional and state health officials, but it would construct a three-story addition to the east and two smaller additions to the north side. A number of departments were enlarged, including a complete revamping of the surgical area, and the hospital was able to add a new cardiac care unit, intensive care unit, and lobby.

In 1982 the John D. Root addition was opened, which gave the hospital a new main entrance off North Elm Avenue. The facility's total size then was more than 62,000 square feet. It had 64 adult medical-surgical beds, 6 in pediatrics, and 5 in intensive care.

Jackson Osteopathic Hospital officials are proud of the fact that none of its expansion programs have required government funding. All construction and renovation has been financed by staff and corporation members' contributions, loans, and charges for services.

Part of the hospital's support comes from its loyal Guild—its women's auxiliary founded in June 1944. Initially headed by Mrs. Alan R. Becker, wife of one of the hospital's founders, the women did much volunteer work for the hospital and raised funds for needed equipment through bake sales and dances. In the 1980s the more than 40 active and associate members continue with a similar purpose, to raise money for hospital needs and to create a better understanding of osteopathy. When a new meditation room was completed, the Guild donated money for a large stained-glass window, carpeting, and furnishings.

Jackson Osteopathic Hospital, which serves Jackson County and parts of Lenawee, Hillsdale, Ingham, and Washtenaw counties, had more than 40 staff and consulting physicians affiliated with it by the mid-1980s. It has encouraged more osteopathic physicians to practice in Jackson by building two nearby two-suite offices. It has begun a cooperative internship program with another osteopathic hospital to give aspiring physicians training in medical and surgical services. It has also expanded its own services by opening a new Doctors Care Center, which provides patients with osteopathic care after physicians' office hours in an evening and weekend clinic.

Jackson Osteopathic Hospital's founding physicians, Dr. Leslie B. Walker (left), and Dr. John D. Root, helped dedicate the hospital's newest addition almost 40 years after the facility first opened.

SPRING ARBOR COLLEGE

Spring Arbor College was founded in 1873 under the auspices of the Free Methodist Church as a seminary, or private academy, teaching elementary and secondary students. Since the 1960s it has evolved into an academically competitive four-year liberal arts institution offering a wide variety of academic programs ranging from the humanities and natural sciences to preprofessional degrees. It offers its programs within a friendly, evangelical Christian community.

As the school catalog states, "Spring Arbor College provides a breadth of academic opportunities which enables its students to prepare for productive and rewarding roles in society." Its faculty, of whom about 40 percent hold doctorate degrees, is committed to academic excellence.

Faculty members are also involved in activities outside the classroom. Dr. David Johnson, a chemistry professor, is conducting research on energy-storage systems for the National Aeronautics and Space

Administration. Dr. David Gillingham, assistant professor of music, has been commissioned to write a composition to be performed by 10 university bands from the Midwest. And Dr. Charles Dillman, professor of religion, is a member of the board of trustees of *The Christian Scholar's Review Board.*

The purpose of a college is the education of students, and the 1,100 attending Spring Arbor certainly have a variety of programs from which to choose. In addition to standard academic courses, Spring Arbor provides other methods of learning.

One option is independent study, which allows a student to pick a topic and research it with tutorial guidance. Foreign study can range from a semester at Bradford University in England to a period of mission service in Haiti. Closer to home, students have the opportunity to study inner-city culture at the Urban Life Center and the Olive Branch Mission in Chicago. Those interested in our political system can spend time at the American Studies Program in Washington, D.C., sponsored by the Christian College Coalition. Biology students can spend a semester at the AuSable Trails Camp for Environ-

mental Study near Mancelona, Michigan. The college also operates extension campuses in downtown Jackson and in Flint, and serves a population of over 200 students at the State Prison of Southern Michigan, just northeast of Jackson.

A particularly innovative approach has been the development of the bachelor of arts in management of human resources degree field-based program. This unique alternative to the traditional method of pursuing a degree is designed for adults who want to earn a degree while on the job, in classes close to home and coordinated with their schedules. The program has experienced rapid growth and presently has extension offices in Jackson, Flint, and Lansing.

Spring Arbor remained a seminary from its founding until 1929 when "Junior College" was added to its name. In 1959 it was announced that the school would become a four-year college. The first class graduated in 1965. Spring Arbor College is fully accredited by the North Central Association of Colleges and Schools.

Spring Arbor College serves approximately 1,100 students—650 on-campus residents and 450 in a variety of external programs. Of the on-campus population, 80 percent come from the state of Michigan.

The Spring Arbor Seminary faculty, students, and staff of the 1882-1883 academic year.

THE OFFICE SUPPLY HOUSE

The Office Supply House in its first (top), 1911, and second (above), 1917, downtown Jackson locations.

In a highly competitive business like selling office supplies and furniture, success is often as dependent on intangibles as it is on product lines. At The Office Supply House, one key to prosperity has been service—good, old-fashioned customer service.

"When my parents bought the business in 1963, it was almost bankrupt," says Paul Rumohr, president of the firm. "They turned it around by actively letting customers know they were there to serve them." Kenneth F. and Dorothy J. Rumohr made sure that customers knew the company's services were available whenever needed—day or night or on weekends. The stores have always carried quality products and developed a reputation as central Michigan's complete office products center.

The Rumohrs bought the firm, then at 129 South Mechanic Street, in order to manage their own business in a field they found interesting. Kenneth Rumohr had been treasurer of a refrigeration company, where one of his duties was to see the salesman who sold office supplies and equipment to the business. Impressed with the possibilities of the office supplies market, he owned one store for about three years, sold it, and later bought The Office Supply House when it became available.

Since the Rumohrs took over, the changes in products offered by The Office Supply House have traced the evolution in modern office operations. Where their products were once ledger sheets, they now sell computer printout forms. Where they sold ink pens, they now carry felt-tip markers and ball-point pens. Adding machines have given way to electronic calculators. And manual typewriters have gone through the electric typewriter phase to be replaced by advanced word processors.

The Rumohrs' success can be measured by the firm's expansion during the 20 years before their retirement in early 1984. Sales went from about $200,000 during their first year of operation to more than one million dollars today. When they took over the company, its floor space was about 4,000 square feet. In the 1970s display space in the Jackson store was doubled, and branch outlets were opened in Ann Arbor and Mason. The Ann Arbor store has since been closed, but the Mason facility has been consolidated into a new Cedar Park outlet in Holt.

In 1979 the Rumohrs made what turned out to be a fortuitous decision when they bought a building at 808 East Michigan Avenue and opened a second Jackson store. Spending more than $220,000 for improvements and additions, they turned it into their new main office, showroom, warehouse, and distribution center, while maintaining the downtown store as well.

In June 1981 a combination of age and heavy rains caused the roof at the rear of the building at 129 South Mechanic Street to collapse. Although the damage to merchandise was minimal, it was decided to demolish the rear portion of the building, sell the remainder of the structure, and move all operations to the East Michigan Avenue site.

Today the 20 employees in the Jackson and Holt stores serve thousands of customers through south-central Michigan. The Office Supply House is changing from a family-owned business to one that uses the talents of many employees in its management as it moves into a new era of high-technology office supply.

C. THORREZ INDUSTRIES, INC.

Far from its roots in the farmland around Flanders, Belgium, C. Thorrez Industries, Inc., has evolved into a leader in the screw machine production field in Jackson. The Belgian immigrants who came to this community just after the turn of the century added to the town's core of hard working people. Many, like the young Camiel Thorrez, were mechanically inclined and began shops.

Thorrez was an innovator in the screw machine industry in the area. Through his efforts, many of the screw machine industrialists here received their training—at one time or another they worked for Thorrez. Now a multimillion-dollar business, C. Thorrez Industries designs, engineers, and produces a wide range of parts for industry. The company manufactures items such as transmission, brake, and engine parts; oil pan plugs; ball studs; office furniture parts and chair spindles; as well as parts for lawn and garden equipment.

Principal customers are Bendix Corporation, Chrysler Corporation, General Motors Corporation, Ford Motor Company, Steelcase, Inc., Wheel Horse, Inc., and Rockwell Standard Corporation. With its two separately owned but affiliated plants in Concord and Stockbridge, C. Thorrez Industries is able to offer its customers full capabilities in screw machine production. While the Jackson plant handles bar stock up to 1.5 inches in diameter, the other two plants produce from stock up to 3.5 inches. This specialization results in efficiency for each plant, and cooperation among the three plants, through subletting of contracts, results in full service for customers.

With annual sales of close to nine million dollars and a work force of about 95 employees, C. Thorrez Industries evolved from earlier companies. Soon after Camiel Thorrez emigrated from Belgium in 1912, he helped start Jackson Screw Machine Company. He left that to help found Thorrez-Maes Manufacturing Company in 1926. Thorrez headed the new screw machine company as president with co-founders Victor Maes as vice-president, and Henry Thorrez, his brother, as treasurer.

Thorrez-Maes operated on Wildwood Avenue for 22 years, producing nuts, bolts, gear blanks, bicycle hubs, automobile door knobs, and brake pins—anything that could be made from a steel or brass bar from one-eighth to 3.5 inches in thickness. Employment increased to 250 workers by 1939 and doubled during World War II, when the firm turned its attention to war work and the manufacture of machine gun bullets, trench mortar bomb parts, base plugs for incendiary bombs, and aircraft engine parts.

A union dispute closed Thorrez-Maes in 1948. Three months after negotiations broke down with UAW-CIO Local 64, the firm announced it would sell its machinery and equipment at auction. Later the plant was sold.

Camiel Thorrez founded a new venture, C. Thorrez Industries, in 1946 with about 20 employees in a small plant at 2001 Spring Arbor Road. Sales that first year were about $800,000, a figure that has increased more than 10 times over. In 1964 the company's current plant was built at 4909 West Michigan Avenue; with a subsequent addition, the plant has about 30,000 square feet of operating space.

Outlasting many other enterprises in town, C. Thorrez Industries, Inc., is another Jackson example of family unity. Camiel's three sons, five grandsons, and two granddaughters now provide second- and third-generation leadership for the almost 40-year-old firm.

C. Thorrez Industries, Inc., a leader in the screw machine production field in Jackson, occupies this facility at 4909 West Michigan.

W.A. FOOTE MEMORIAL HOSPITAL

When W.A. Foote Memorial Hospital opened the doors of its new facility in June 1983, it added a new concept to health care in Jackson. Health care, in keeping with its trustees' philosophy, would be provided not only compassionately and efficiently, but also with up-to-date equipment in a modern facility.

The 12th-largest hospital in Michigan, Foote is comprised of a four-wing, seven-story new building and several ancillary units. The $69-million project has resulted in a facility with 428 medical-surgical beds and an additional 60 mental health and alcohol rehabilitation beds.

Its staff consists of nearly 170 physicians, and its payroll has approximately 1,700 full- and part-time employees. The hospital aids in the training of new generations of medical personnel through program affiliations with Jackson Community College, Western Michigan University, and Eastern Michigan University.

Such facilities and programs are a giant leap from the origins of health care in Jackson. The community's first recognized hospital, the Jackson City Hospital, opened in 1888, with a bed capacity of 15, at 1501 East Ganson Street, now the John George Home for Men.

In 1915, following the illness and death of her husband, Mrs. W.A. Foote noted the overcrowded conditions at the hospital—which then had 50 beds—and donated the present site on North East Street, just north of Michigan Avenue for a new hospital. The 100-bed W.A. Foote Memorial Hospital was completed in 1918.

In 1929 a 45-bed annex was built through the contributions of Captain and Mrs. William Sparks, longtime community leaders. Around 1960 a new wing was

constructed, bringing the total bed capacity to 270, with 44 bassinets.

Meanwhile, across town another medical facility was developing. In 1915 Mercy Hospital was opened, at 115 North Blackstone Street, by the Roman Catholic Sisters of Mercy. Three years later a new Mercy Hospital with a capacity of 75 beds was erected on Lansing Avenue. Expansions brought patient capacity to 205 beds, plus 40 bassinets.

Almost since its beginning, Foote Hospital was owned by the City of Jackson. However, after lengthy community deliberations, in 1974 the operation of Foote Hospital was placed in the hands of the Jackson Hospital Authority, and a private, nonprofit corporation was formed to lease the hospital facilities and operate them for the benefit of the public.

In 1975 the Sisters of Mercy decided to discontinue their operations in Jackson and sold their facility for $2.5 million to the trustees of W.A. Foote Memorial Hospital. Mercy Hospital became Foote Hospital West. It continued to operate until the newly constructed Foote Memorial Hospital was opened in June 1983, and, later, as an ancillary facility.

With approximately 100 years of permanent, established hospital care in the community, Jackson residents can take pride in the history of medical treatment that has been provided locally. Now, with the new

The nursing station is surrounded by numerous treatment rooms in the emergency area, where over 50,000 people were treated in 1983. The concept of locating the nursing station in the center allows the staff easy access to the treatment rooms. Beth Singer—Photographer.

Foote Memorial Hospital facilities, they can also look forward to improved medical care in the years to come.

The new, 428-bed Foote Memorial Hospital opened its doors to the public on June 25, 1983, after two hospitals had combined eight years earlier. This full-service facility ranks as the 12th-largest hospital in Michigan and the second-largest employer in Jackson. Beth Singer—Photographer.

WYMAN-GORDON COMPANY MIDWEST DIVISION/JACKSON

The name has changed a number of times over the years, but the principal product has always remained the same—crankshafts for over-the-highway trucks, heavy industry, farm equipment, and the military. Wyman-Gordon Company's Midwest Division operation in Jackson has been an established force in the crankshaft machining industry since 1914.

Today Wyman-Gordon, whose Midwest Division also includes two plants in Illinois, is the largest independent crankshaft machiner in the United States. The Jackson plant produces about 80,000 crankshafts yearly for customers such as the Detroit Diesel Allison Division of General Motors, Caterpillar Tractor, Ford Motor Company, Deere & Co., and International Harvester. In addition, in 1984 the plant was awarded a major automotive crankshaft-machining contract by Chevrolet.

With a $23-million expansion of its plant at 2218 East High Street that included $16 million in state-of-the-art machining equipment, Wyman-Gordon in Jackson began the 1980s with facilities that will be up-to-date in the 1990s.

The plant is equipped with four Cincinnati Milacron lathes and four American GFM internal mills. These can take a crankshaft, forged at one of the other Midwest Division plants, and begin machining it. The piece is then sent to the plant's induction-hardening machinery for

heat treating. The finishing process involves grinding and lapping. Wyman-Gordon/Jackson has six Warner & Swasey hub grinders, two Landis fully automatic pin grinders, and six Newall grinders, along with four Impco lapping machines.

Because of the precise requirements of its customers, Wyman-Gordon uses statistical process controls in its machining work. At every step along the manufacturing line, the crankshaft is statistically checked and the examinations are charted to ensure that the product meets customer blueprint specifications.

Customers are also demanding better quality. In the past, many diesel engine manufacturers warranted their engines for 200,000 miles. Now it is 300,000 miles and the target is 500,000.

Those customer requirements are basically no different than they were in 1914, when the Jackson Motorshaft Company began operations after its owners moved here from Hastings, Michigan, where they had begun business in 1910. Headquarters and principal manufacturing facilities were located at 2314 Tyson Street and remained there until operations were consolidated in the expanded 250,000-square-foot facilities on High Street in 1981. The Tyson Street operation, which eventually

Crankshafts, whether for trucks, heavy industry, farm equipment, or the military, have been the firm's principal product since 1914.

became Plant 1, contained 140,000 square feet of manufacturing space and at times employed over 600 workers.

In 1927 Jackson Motorshaft manufactured crankshafts for the first Model T Ford and two years later for the first Model A. The 1930s saw crankshafts machined for the Huppmobile and later for the Pierce Arrow. In 1940 the firm began making crankshafts for the Packard-built Rolls Royce engines that powered the legendary Navy PT boats in World War II.

In 1936 Jackson became the first crankshaft machiner to utilize induction hardening, which has now become a universally accepted practice on crankshaft-bearing surfaces. The "Tocco" machine at Plant No. 1 bore the serial number one, signifying it was the first in existence.

In 1929 the firm was purchased by Muskegon Motor Specialties Company and became its Jackson Crankshaft division. The parent organization ran into financial difficulties in the early 1960s. To prevent the closing of the Jackson Crankshaft facilities, a group of about 20 local men bought control of the business in 1964 and

Wyman-Gordon Company, Midwest Division/Jackson is located at 2218 East High Street. Drawing by Valerie Brower, 1982.

reorganized it to satisfy federal court requirements.

Wyman-Gordon acquired a one-third interest in the firm in 1967 and completed its takeover in 1974. Wyman-Gordon Company, headquartered in Worcester, Massachusetts, was founded in 1883. It is engaged principally in the engineering, production, and marketing of technically advanced forgings, and is also a prominent builder of heavy-duty equipment for large-scale agricultural and earth-moving applications.

In 1975 the local firm's name was formally changed to the Jackson Crankshaft Company, and in 1982 it became Wyman-Gordon Company, Midwest Division/ Jackson.

It was but a short step from near bankruptcy to expansion. By 1969 the firm bought and added on to an existing building on High Street in the Micor Industrial Park. It became Plant No. 2. In 1979 Wyman-Gordon/Jackson announced it would close its aged facilities on Tyson Street and consolidate all operations at Plant No. 2.

Throughout the years, the Jackson shop has been recognized for its developmental work. It has supplied numerous prototype crankshafts to most of the nation's major engine builders. Those crankshafts were used in experimental engines and new models in various stages of development and testing. About 20 of its 400 salaried and hourly workers are employed in the development of prototypes. One of their major efforts in recent years has been the development of a crankshaft for a new Series 60

Formerly known as Plant No. 2, the present facility on East High Street is the only Wyman-Gordon plant in Jackson since the 2314 Tyson plant was closed.

heavy-duty engine to be produced by Detroit Diesel in the mid-1980s. heavy-duty engine produced by Detroit Diesel in the mid-1980s.

The Jackson Motorshaft predecessor to Wyman-Gordon/Jackson went into business directing its efforts to the manufacture of

An interior view of the 1981 additon to the plant.

high-quality, fully machined crankshafts. That direction has not changed. Throughout its history, the company has maintained a reputation for quality, advanced production techniques, and innovative thinking.

Floyd "Porky" Redmond working at a Leland-Gifford machine at old Plant No. 1, located at 2314 Tyson Street. Photo circa 1958.

JACKSON FORGE CORPORATION

When Jackson Drop Forge Company was purchased in 1982 and renamed Jackson Forge Corporation, the firm received an infusion of enthusiastic support from its new owners, who announced they were "solidly pro-Jackson, pro-Michigan, pro-Midwest."

William H. Rentschler, John H. Altorfer, and Thomas J. Houser comprise Greenwood Industries, the corporate entity that bought the Jackson concern from the families of its original founders.

The new owners instituted the new name to reflect the company's broadened range of products. Not just a producer of drop forgings, Jackson Forge manufactures an extensive line of steel forgings ranging from 2 to 180 pounds in size. It makes parts for farm implements, light and heavy trucks, and off-road and industrial equipment. It also supplies some parts to the automobile and petrochemical industries. Primary customers are Chrysler Corporation, Cummins Engine, Mack Truck, Rockwell International, and Dana.

Jackson Drop Forge Company, located at 2001 Wellworth, was begun in 1945 by a small group of Jackson men experienced in forge work. The new operation grew steadily, and in its 11th year required a $2-million expansion program to double its production capacity and to diversify its product line. An all-steel forging building was completed and stocked with $400,000 in new machines and equipment as the first part of that expansion program. Construction of a large steel-cleaning room, enclosing of shipping dock facilities, and the installation of an overhead crane in the dock area completed the program.

Before the firm expanded its capacity, it was about 80-percent dependent on the automobile industry. When production increased considerably, forging of auto industry parts made up only about 20 percent of the Jackson Drop Forge market. The remaining production was supplied to the plumbing, materials-handling, earth-moving, railroad, truck, aircraft, farm, and textile industries.

Another expansion followed in 1962. Approximately 11,000 square feet of press plant, die shop, and office facilities were added, allowing the company to increase its capacity by about one-third, and permitting the addition of more workers in the 57,500-square-foot operation. By 1971 Jackson Drop Forge had become one of the leading closed-die forging job shops in the Midwest, and it had grown from 25 to 250 employees.

When Greenwood Industries purchased the firm, it was down to 75 employees, reflecting the downturn in the economy. The new owners retained company management and set as their goals aggressive sales, a return to full employment, and expansion. Employment has since risen to nearly 150 workers. When the Clark Equipment Company forging plant on Tyson Street was closed, Jackson Forge purchased toolings, dies, and other equipment to help ensure that many forging orders would continue to be produced in Jackson. The new equipment put about 300 additional products—either original equipment or after-market—into the Jackson Forge product line.

Sales, which hovered around the $11-million mark annually in the recession years of 1982 and 1983, turned upward with a projected $18-million figure for 1984, and higher rates are expected in the years to come. Banking on an upturn in Michigan's economy, the three owners of Jackson Forge Corporation refer to themselves as "the good-news guys—the ones who are going to be staying and expanding."

ELLA SHARP MUSEUM

"Hillside," a busy family farm in the late 1800s, is now one of Jackson's finest cultural and recreational resources.

Purchased in 1855 by Abraham Wing of New York for his widowed daughter, Mary Farnsworth, the land was developed into a model farm of some 800 acres by Mary and her second husband, Dwight Merriman. The only one of the Merrimans' four children to survive was their daughter, Ella, born in 1857.

After Ella's marriage in 1881 to John C. Sharp, the couple took over management of the farm. Sharp, a lawyer and one-term state senator, died in 1908, and Ella in 1912. Her local and statewide interests in civic improvement and conservation led her to will her house to the City of Jackson for a museum and a sizable portion of her farm as a city park. The park became a reality in 1915.

It took until 1964 for Mrs. Sharp's wish for a museum to be fulfilled. The Jackson Junior Welfare League had been working to establish a community museum and discovered

In 1968 the Peter F. Hurst Planetarium was completed, honoring the association's first president.

the legacy. A fund-raising campaign was successful in acquiring enough money to renovate the house and provide an operating budget for the museum's first few years. The city deeded the house and five acres of land to the museum association for 99 years.

Ella Sharp Museum's founders planned it as a historical museum to tell Jackson's long and colorful history. The Merriman-Sharp family had left enough personal effects to provide a record of the way of life in the late 1800s. The house was refurbished, furnished with the family's decorative art and furniture, and dedicated on October 3, 1965.

From its beginning it has been a community organization. It receives no local tax money; it is supported primarily by memberships, contributions, and bequests.

Chief among its educational efforts are the Pioneer Living and Arts Go To School programs. Elementary school students are able to learn firsthand how pioneer children lived, played, and went to school, using the authentically restored and furnished one-room Dibble School and log cabin. Both were donated and moved onto museum grounds. Arts Go To School is an outreach program in which volunteer docents take art and artifacts into the schoolroom for class discussion in the arts and humanities.

The museum's master plan called for the addition of new buildings as funds were available. In 1968 the Peter F. Hurst Planetarium and the Gallery were completed, thus honoring the association's first president. The Gallery houses the museum's rotating exhibitions in the arts and humanities. In 1970 the facility opened one of the farm buildings as a pioneer-era general store, and the Art Studio addition to the Gallery was completed in 1974, adding a new area especially designed for fine art and historic craft classes.

The Ella, as the museum is affectionately known, required an updated growth plan by 1980. New geographical boundaries were established to allow for future expansion, and the museum was able to restore more of the farm buildings along Farm Lane as the city turned over this properly to the museum association.

The facility's staff, trustees, and members take pride in the fact that Ella Sharp Museum is accredited by the American Association of Museums. It has fulfilled the goals of its originators by providing a home for historic materials and memorabilia, as well as enriching the cultural and artistic experiences of Jackson's citizens.

The Ella Sharp museum complex.

GLICK IRON AND METAL COMPANY

When you drive past Glick Iron and Metal Company on your way into Jackson, the route that takes you to the central business district is named Louis Glick Highway, in honor of the man who was prominent as a businessman and philanthropist.

In 1916 Louis Glick arrived in Jackson with $800, a sledgehammer, and a chisel. He had operated a scrap-iron business in Niles with a brother-in-law and planned to do the same here. Along with his few tools, the young man, born in Budapest, Hungary, and raised in Saginaw, brought with him a business sense that helped him expand from a small, five-man scrap-metal firm to the large, thriving business it is today. Though Louis Glick died in 1967, his son and grandson have carried on the family business.

Machinery is the key to the growth of Glick Iron. In his first year of operation, Louis Glick and another worker broke up automobile bodies with hand tools. By the time his son, Robert A., joined the firm in 1936, Glick Iron

Louis Glick, founder.

Robert A. Glick, chairman of the board.

had a few trucks and had acquired an alligator shear—a $5,000 piece of equipment that cuts metal into small pieces.

Even then, men worked with shovels, pitchforks, and wheelbarrows, loading scrap-metal pieces into trucks and railroad cars by hand—it took two men nearly three days to load a railroad car. Glick Iron bought its first crane in about 1940, and with a modern crane, a railroad car is now loaded in one and a half hours.

Starting small, the company moved from one location to another, acquiring land and spreading out. It now fills about 25 acres along Airline Drive on the city's southeast side, with headquarters at 701 Lewis Street.

Glick Iron helps fill the demands of steel mills throughout the Midwest for quality scrap to refine and melt down into new metals, a cheaper process for them than starting with ore from mines. The process also serves to recycle automobiles, home appliances,

worn-out farm machinery, and the metal scrap that is left over when industry makes its products.

In a good year the firm processes 100,000 tons, prepared and cut into pieces according to its customers' requirements. Some want two-foot scraps; some want smaller or larger pieces. Some want only new materials; some require used metals.

Recycling all it can, Glick Iron salvages motors from cars and sorts and processes other, nonferrous metals—copper, brass, aluminum, and stainless steel.

In the Glick Iron scrapbook, a 1923 income statement shows sales of $131,000. Today those sales have multiplied many times over. The firm's newest major piece of equipment is a $750,000, hydraulically operated steel shear that compresses metal scrap and cuts it into pieces of any length.

Robert A. Glick is now chairman of the board and his son, Carlton L., is president. In addition to managing the firm, the family carries on Louis' tradition of helping others through low-interest student loans from the Louis Glick Trust.

Carlton L. Glick, president.

KELSEY-HAYES COMPANY

The Kelsey-Hayes Company was founded in 1927, through the merger of two firms that had separately achieved great success in the manufacture of wood-spoked wheels. Jacksonian Clarence B. Hayes was the producer of nearly two-thirds of all automotive wheels, and Detroiter John Kelsey, who had entered the wheel business to supply Henry Ford's young company, had gone on to manufacture wheels for World War I military wagons and gun carriages.

Hayes Wheel and Kelsey Wheel were merged when the industry shifted its demands—modern wire wheels were developed, and manufacturers had to revamp their production to survive. In 1927 the new enterprise acquired the necessary wire-wheel patents, and its Jackson plant at 512 North Wisner Street was at full production.

Though Kelsey-Hayes began as a supplier to the automobile industry, and the Jackson operation is part of the Romulus-based corporation's Automotive Division, production here was diversified for many years. In 1939 farm tractor rims and wheels were first produced, and during World War II the plant produced equipment for the military.

A decade later, the firm entered the aircraft industry. Jackson workers produced power recovery units (turbo-charger) for Curtiss-Wright piston engines, made component parts for military jet engines, and helped develop the first lightweight jet aircraft.

Needing more space for aircraft parts production, Kelsey-Hayes bought its West Complex at 1600 Wildwood Avenue. The Wisner Street facility is now known as the East Complex. A third facility—at 2300 Leroy—was opened by the company in 1950, but is now idle.

Despite previous diversification, automotive production has always

The Kelsey-Hayes Company's original facility at 512 North Wisner Street is now known as the East Complex.

been a staple of Kelsey-Hayes' manufacturing in Jackson. Hydraulic brakes were added to the product line in 1939, and after World War II the business consolidated its entire drum brake production operations in Jackson. Drum brake production continued in the community until the early 1980s. In 1946 the Jackson plants entered the recreational vehicle field with the manufacture of electric brakes for mobile homes and trailers, and became their number-one supplier.

By 1964 Kelsey-Hayes saw its years of research and development of disc brakes reach fruition. It began production in Jackson of the disc brakes that became standard on many passenger cars and trucks. By the early 1970s the West Complex had become—and still is—the largest independent producer of original-equipment disc brakes in the world.

Disc brakes and front wheel hubs are the firm's biggest products in the 1980s, along with brake-control valve bodies. Ford Motor Company is its major customer, followed by AMC-Renault, Chrysler Corporation, and Volkswagen.

In 1973, the year Kelsey-Hayes merged with Fruehauf Corporation, the pioneer truck trailer manufacturer, sales from Jackson plants averaged $7.7 million a month and more than 1,000 salaried and hourly persons were employed. Ten years later, reflecting the depths of Michigan's early 1980s recession, sales were just over $4.5 million a month. By 1984, however, sales were averaging $6.2 million monthly, and were expected to climb. Employment, too, was steadily rising, from an average of just over 325 in 1983 to nearly 370 the next year.

Needing more space for aircraft parts production, Kelsey-Hayes purchased this building at 1600 Wildwood Avenue; it is now known as its West Complex.

LEFERE FORGE AND MACHINE COMPANY

At Lefere Forge and Machine Company, business has always been a family affair. All of its chief executives have been sons and grandsons of the founders. And its next generation of leaders is being trained on the work floor of this fabricator of parts for vehicle manufacturers.

The firm, still operating at its original Hupp Avenue location, produces ring gears, companion flanges, hubs, and universal joints for such manufacturers as Budd Company, Motor Wheel, Rockwell International, Clark Equipment, and Allied Chucker.

Its focus has changed little since its founding. The company initially produced parts for passenger cars, then for trucks, and still later for road building and farm equipment. By the 1980s Lefere Forge had discontinued passenger car parts production to concentrate on parts for heavier vehicles.

Alidor and Henry Lefere were born in Belgium and came to the United States in 1905. Alidor, then 19 and already a skilled machinist, worked a few weeks for low pay in Detroit before coming to Jackson where his first job paid him the higher wage of one dollar a day, with another worker translating his Belgian language. He held a number of machinist jobs, and from 1908 to 1910 he operated the Lefere Machine Shop and helped

Lefere Forge and Machine Company's original facilities at 665 Hupp Avenue in 1929.

organize the Riverside Forge and Machine Company four years later.

In 1929 the two Lefere brothers set up the Lefere Forge and Machine Company with Alidor as president and Henry as vice-president. They began operations on June 28, 1929, with a forge shop, tool and die room, and modern office building on just over nine acres at 665 Hupp Avenue. The firm's 85 employees, working one shift, were able to produce 154,000 pounds of steel parts.

Lefere Forge and Machine was one of the Jackson firms that defied the Depression, though business fell off considerably during the early 1930s. In January 1933 the company was employing only a few men, sometimes working a four-day week,

but by the following year the plant was again running steadily.

Over the years Lefere Forge and Machine has increased to three times its original work space, with the latest addition built in 1952. Today it has 10 hammers, ranging in size from 2,500 to 8,000 pounds, and two high-production presses, providing a one-shift output of 180,000 pounds.

Sons, grandsons, and other descendants of the two Lefere brothers have always provided the primary leadership for the company. Founder Alidor served as president until 1946, then as chairman of the board until his death in 1959.

His eldest son, Maurice P., succeeded him in the presidency until his death in 1954, and the next born, Albert V., until 1981. Royal P. "Ike," as the next son in line, was then elected president by the board of directors.

Tradition requires that all executives at Lefere Forge and Machine Company be capable of doing any job in the plant, which takes about 15 years to learn. The newest generation of Leferes is hard at work now, learning this family business.

Initially producing parts for passenger cars, Lefere Forge and Machine changed its focus to parts for heavier vehicles. It has grown at the same location, as evidenced by this 1982 photo.

*Streetcars which ran between downtown
Jackson and Vandercook Lake brought
thousands to Hague Park and helped make it
a favorite summertime attraction. The
"bedspring" contraption on the front of the
car could be dropped to the level of the
tracks to scoop up obstacles or fallen people.
(MHC, BHL, UM)*

An estimated 125,000 people jammed Jackson
streets for a parade honoring James A.
McDivitt, Jr., on June 16, 1965. McDivitt, a
1950 graduate of Jackson Junior College, was
command pilot of the 62-orbit Gemini 4
flight. McDivitt later commanded Apollo 9.
Courtesy, Jackson Citizen Patriot

PATRONS

PATRONS
The following individuals, companies, and organizations have made a valuable commitment to the quality of this publication. Windsor Publications and the Greater Jackson Chamber of Commerce gratefully acknowledge their participation in *Jackson: An Illustrated History.*

ADCO Products, Inc.*
Brail/Winzeler Dry Cleaners
Brooklyn Products Inc.
Burton Abstract Division-First
   American Title Insurance Co.
Camp International, Inc.*
Camshaft Machine Company*
City of Jackson Water Department*
Comerica Bank-Jackson*
Commonwealth Associates Inc.*
Consumers Power Company*
Dawn Food Products, Inc.*
Dermatology Clinic of Jackson
Dick J. Dijkman, D.D.S., M.S., P.C.
DI-TEC MOLD CORPORATION
Art Dolan Inc.
A.G. Edwards & Sons, Inc.
Mr. & Mrs. Robert H. Emmons
Fab-Alloy Company
W.A. Foote Memorial Hospital*
Glick Iron and Metal Company*
R.A. Greene Wastewater Treatment
   Plant*
Hall & Kennedy Inc.
Happy Hunters Antique Club
Harris-McBurney Company*
Philip E. Hoffman, State
   Representative, 23rd District
Holiday Inn of Jackson
Horton House
Inn on Jackson Square*
Jackson Business Institute*
Jackson Community College
Jackson County Farm Bureau
Jackson District Library
Jackson Forge Corporation*
Jackson Harness Raceway
Jackson Junior Welfare League
Jackson Osteopathic Hospital*
Jacobson Stores Inc.*
Kaywood Products Corporation

Kelsey-Hayes Company*
Lefere Forge and Machine
   Company*
Dr. & Mrs. Roger G. Lyons
Mary Mackie McVicker
MARBEN MANUFACTURING
   DIVISION-SIMPSON INDUSTRIES,
   INC.
Marcoux, Allen & Beaman, P.C.
R.J. Michaels, Inc.
Michigan Bank-Midwest
Michigan International Speedway*
Ray & Elaine Miller
The Office Supply House*
Patch, McClafferty & Anderson,
   P.C.-Attorneys at Law
Photo Marketing Association
   International
Pioneer Foundry Company, Inc.
Ella Sharp Museum*
SNF Co. Inc.
Spring Arbor College*
C. Thorrez Industries, Inc.*
Mr. & Mrs. M.B. Townsend, Jr., in
   memory of Charlotte A.
   Townsend
L.E. Warren, Inc.
The Wetherby Company, Funeral
   Directors
Willbee Concrete Products &
   Willbee Transit Mix Company,
   Inc.*
Jim Winter Buick-GMC-Datsun, Inc.
Rick Wyatt Tree Service
Wyman-Gordon Company
Midwest Division/Jackson*

*Partners in Progress of *Jackson: An Illustrated History.* The histories of these companies and organizatons appear in Chapter 6, beginning on page 89.

BIBLIOGRAPHY

Albion Catalog, 1977-78. Albion, Michigan: Albion College, 1977.

Art Work of Jackson, Michigan. Chicago: The W.H. Parish Publishing Co., 1894.

Atkin, Glenn. "Goose Lake." Supplement to the *Jackson Citizen Patriot,* August 15, 1970.

Bacon, Ila J. "The State Prison of Southern Michigan, 1837-1959." Unpublished manuscript, 1959. In Jackson District Library.

Barger, Melvin D. *The JBU Story.* Jackson: Jackson Business University, 1967.

Bush, George. *Future Builders: The Story of Michigan's Consumers Power Company.* New York: McGraw-Hill Book Co., 1973.

Chamberlain, John. *Freedom and Independence: The Hillsdale Story.* Hillsdale, Michigan: College Press, 1979.

Combination Atlas Map of Jackson County. Chicago: Everts & Stewart, 1874.

Coolidge, Ruth E. *Pioneering in Education.* Jackson: Jackson Community College, 1967.

Cowden, George M. "Newspaper History in Jackson, Michigan." Unpublished paper, 1962. In Jackson Citizen Patriot library.

DeLand, Charles V. *Deland's History of Jackson County, Michigan.* n.p.: B.F. Bowen, 1903.

DeLind, Dr. Laura B. *Jackson: The First One Hundred Years, 1829-1929.* n.p.: Ella Sharp Museum Association of Jackson, n.d.

Delphian '65: Jackson Community College 1965 Yearbook. Jackson: Jackson Community College, 1965.

Dunbar, Willis F. and Shade, William G. "The Black Man Gains the Vote: The Centennial of Impartial Suffrage in Michigan," *Michigan History,* vol. LVI, no. 1, Spring 1972.

_____. *Michigan Through the Centuries,* vol. I. New York: Lewis Historical Publishing Company, Inc., 1955.

Emens, Mary F. "A Brief History of the Theater of Jackson, Michigan." Unpublished paper, 1961. In Jackson District Library.

Greater Jackson Chamber of Commerce. *Greater Jackson, Michigan.* Encino, California: Windsor Publications Inc., 1971.

Green, Nellie Blair. "Jackson County History." A series of articles from the *Jackson Tribune,* August 2, 1929, to February 14, 1930.

Haney, Bill. *From Spirit Lake to Goose Lake.* Grass Lake, Michigan: The New Press, 1971.

Headlight Jackson Michigan: Sights and Scenes Along the Michigan Central Line, vol. 2, no. 7. Chicago: Photo-Engraving Company, 1895.

History of Jackson County, Michigan. Chicago: Inter-state Publishing Co., 1881.

Jackson Citizen Patriot, 1918 —. Daily newspaper, title varies.

Jackson Junior Welfare League. "Community Research Papers," Unpublished papers, 1963. In Jackson District Library.

Jackson, Michigan. Jackson: Jackson Citizen Press, 1912.

Kobs, Peter Lynch. "The Chain of Vindication: Prison Labor, Railroad Conspiracy, and the Fusion of Antislavery in Jackson County, Michigan 1829-1870." Bachelor's thesis, Brown University, 1980.

Morgan, Lucy Stowe. Untitled and unpublished letter to her family in Connecticut, 1831. In Bentley Historical Library, University of Michigan.

Morris, David D. *Lansing, Jackson, Ann Arbor and Automobiles.* Ann Arbor: Edward Brothers, 1976.

Noll, J.E. Untitled summary of the history of the *Jackson Citizen Patriot,* n.d. In Jackson Citizen Patriot library.

Nye, Russel B. "Emerson in Michigan and the Northwest," *Michigan History,* vol. XXVI, 1942.

Peck, Paul R. *Early They Came.* n.p.: Liberty Town Press, 1978.

Pioneer Collections. Collections and Researches made by the Michigan Pioneer and Historical Society including Reports of Officers and Papers Read at the Annual Meeting of 1888. vol. XIII. Lansing: Wynkoop Hallenbeck Crawford Company, 1908.

Pioneer Collections. Michigan Pioneer and Historical Society. vol. XXXV. Lansing: Wynkoop Hallenbeck Crawford Company, 1907.

Pioneer Collections. Michigan Pioneer and Historical Society. vol. XXXVIII. Lansing: Wynkoop Hallenbeck Crawford Company, 1912.

Proctor, Hazel, ed. *Old Jackson Town.* n.p.: Great Lakes Federal Savings, 1981.

Ray, David and Zaski, Jon. *A Picture History of Jackson County, Michigan.* n.p.: Colonial Press, Inc., 1977.

Reed, Lula A. *The Early History, Settlement and Growth of Jackson, Michigan.* n.p.: Reprinted by the Jackson County Historical Society, 1965.

Santer, Richard Arthur. "A Historical Geography of Jackson, Michigan: A Study of the Changing Character of an American City 1829-1969." Ph.D. dissertation, Michigan State University, 1970.

Schram, Donald F., and Gall, Ralph. "The Strange Case of the Eight Deaths and the Frightened Boy." Manuscript copy of a story published in the *Detroit Free Press,* March 21, 1943. In Jackson Citizen Patriot library.

Smith, Ed F. "Well, Anyhow —," A series of columns from the

Jackson Citizen Patriot, February 9, 1941, to January 18, 1953.

Snyder, Howard A. *One Hundred Years at Spring Arbor: A History of Spring Arbor College 1873-1973.* n.p., n.d.

"Sparton Bomb Shell," vol. II, no. 7. Sparks-Withington Company, 1943.

Stocking, William, ed. *Under the Oaks: Commemorating the Fiftieth Anniversary of the Founding of the Republican Party at Jackson, Michigan, July 6, 1854.* Detroit: Detroit Tribune, 1904.

Stone, Harold A., Price, Don K., and Stone, Kathryn H. *City Manager Government in Nine Cities.* Chicago: Public Administration Services, 1940.

Terman, William J. *Spring Arbor Township 1830-1980: Reminiscing Thru a Hundred and Fifty Years.* n.p.: Taylor Publishing Company, 1980.

Totten, Paul H. *Old-Time Brooklyn: A Pictorial History of the Brooklyn Area.* Brooklyn, Michigan: The Exponent Press, 1971.

"Urban Renewal Projects in Michigan." *Michigan Municipal Review,* vol. 36, no. 5. Ann Arbor: Michigan Municipal League, 1963.

Writers Program of the Works Projects Administration. *Michigan: A Guide to the Wolverine State.* New York: Oxford University Press, 1941.

Wyatt, Kenneth John. "That Vile Invective: A History of Partisan Journalism in Jackson County 1837-1866." Master's thesis, Michigan State University, 1976.

Yoss, Fred L. *The Legal History of the Union School District of the City of Jackson.* Jackson: Union School District Board of Education, 1940.

————. *Historic Greater Jackson.* Unpublished paper, 1961. In Jackson District Library.

The mail carriers of 1904 gathered in front of the post office at the southwest corner of Mechanic Street and Washington Avenue for this photograph. The first mail to Jackson came from Ann Arbor in 1830 in the top of a man's hat. The first regular carrier was George Mayo in 1831. (MHC, BHL, UM)

INDEX

Motorized wheels of every kind changed life forever in Jackson. This threesome, pictured about 1920, was evidently prepared for a brisk and muddy spin around town just for fun. Courtesy, Frank Machnik Collection